A TINCTURE OF TIME

by Everett W. Vreeland, DVM

Printed in the USA by

MORRIS PUBLISHING

3212 East Highway 30 • Kearney, NE 68847 • 1-800-650-7888

This book is dedicated to my wife, Nancy, who is my beloved "brown haired girl." She toiled on this writing and has taught me so much of the ingredients and nuances of love.

Also, to the animals from whom I learned so many things about life.

Introduction

I hope the reader will understand that the text that follows, covering a week, took place over about 20 years of my life. A great deal more of the same filled another 20 and I am convinced, with very few exceptions, that I always stood where I was meant to be. It is a very powerful thing to know at an early age what you want to be. It is a very lucky thing to bring it about.

Many stories lie within me and I was often tempted to expand on them but I wished to pinpoint none of the characters warmly hidden here amidst smoke and mirrors. Errors that taught me are left out.

My intention is to show that a useful, fullfilled, and happy life is possible by staying focused--even during detours. Your mind must be wide open and receptive as a youth or you are destined for mediocrity.

I wish to thank John and Pat Noneman for expert help on the cover and Dorothy Ripley for her encouragement at the start.

The critique supplied by Prof. Edward Ives was vital, welcome, and professionally applied. He would make a great surgeon.

I am proud and grateful that my cherished children, Nancy and Dick, moved rapidly to independent and productive lives. I salute them--I hug them!!

CHAPTER ONE: Sunday Night

Blood: Its raw, fresh, sometimes metallic smell filled my car as the door closed heralding, I hoped, the end of a frustrating, tiring, and typically absorbing day. Outside was the muddy barnyard atop a 1600 ft. New England hill drenched in whirling fog and cold, cold rain. The panel lights revealed blood and mucous smeared on white coveralls and my nose rebelled at the concentration of odors -- manure, silage, medicines in the back, and my dog as she slept in the other bucket seat oblivious to her rampant intestinal gas while, to me, it seemed to melt my seat covers. Love may be blind but other senses never sleep.

Smells are a really ubiquitous part of my life, but blood on white stirred more intermittent memory......white chickens leaping and spurting blood after decapitation by ax at Grandfather's farm, splotches of gore on coral sand as we fought our way over a Pacific beach, vivid scarlet on white sheets after a night of passion with a laid back lady who thought more of me than the moon. Blood on the tiled post-mortem floor, vermilion vestiges of a boy's white rabbits torn asunder by dogs of the night and left for viewing from a bedroom window at dawn-- red encircled denim around a jagged bullet hole in a friend's back lying behind his tractor face down in clover plus blood from lives I take in the hunt field, and blood that covers me from the lives I save----or lose.

I settled back to drive the ten miles home relishing the power of my vehicle and feeling in my fingertips the strength and confidence that comes from years of guiding a powerful machine in all phases of weather, light, and road conditions. I had elected not to change coveralls because it was late and I would leave the garment in the clinic tub for the girls to care for in the morning - in spite of their complaint about adding to their work. Then I would head for the hot shower because the frigid wetness from my last effort, complicated bovine obstetrics, was soaking through and grasping my 98° skin with 20° claws.

The reflections about blood had flicked through my mind in less than five seconds and now in another flicker I thought how much better the world would be if more people truly understood, by necessity, the value of a hot shower as opposed to paying for a "sauna"; the satisfaction of fresh spring water when their thirst is such that they don't need an exotic concoction to satisfy and the warmth of a simple car heater that surrounds them when they are really cold.

I also feel that if New York City had taken just a few bombs in World War Two, contemporary thinking in the United States would be vastly improved.

This particular call I had just finished was initiated by an insensitive farmer who had watched the cow since four in the afternoon when he started milking and had done nothing until ten that night when darkness closes in and fear replaces bravado in most diurnal humans. I had actually stopped working for the man five years before because he took too long to pay -- as long as six or seven months. Ask the man why he didn't call me any more and he will give you any one of a myriad of answers, but in ninety percent of these cases the reason is money. Tonight he had pleaded with me to come.

I was ushered into the barn on arrival by a purple-lipped, wall-eyed, unshaven, boozed-up excuse for a man whose life consisted of eating three meals in silence at his employer's table, shoveling manure all day, taking out his frustrations on cows, then retiring to a filthy room in back of the house with a bottle of cheap whiskey.

"Got no girls witcha tonight, Doc?" my usher asked as we walked down the misty, poorly lit alley between the cows.

"Nope," I replied, "they are mostly fair weather types. I think a few of them would have come if they had known I was going to see you."

"Christ!," he exclaimed. "I'd sure like to toss the meat to that one with the long blond hair!"

A reply from me was lost because I was thinking of the rebuttal to that last remark that would have come from "long, blond hair"! I know that this simple man would have been verbally augured in his tracks by what I know to be a fast thinking, pornographically informed mind.

"Would you mind getting my pail full of warm water?" I requested as we were passing the milk room.

"Shore as hell, Doc," he said. "Do you want anything in it?"

"No. It's already there," I said as I searched further down the line for my patient.

3

"Huh?" he answered, because even though he was talking to me at the time, he never saw me pour in the disinfectant.

At the end of the row of animals I found an unfortunate mother collapsed backwards into the manure-filled drop behind her and hung tightly by her head in the stanchion. Extending from her vulva were the two front legs of a calf with baling twine attached by which the man had been hauling. It was called "applying traction" at Cornell. I released her head as my sexy friend returned with the water. The animals eyes were filled with fear and pain, but still, when I scratched her ear in a human attempt to comfort, she quite naturally tried to get me with her horns.

"Goddam ole bitch!" came from behind me and as I proceeded to work I could see what the cow had been through since four in the afternoon. Swearing and violence in this type of person stems from frustration and fear of the unknown. He had been blindly pulling on the two front legs for hours when delivery was impossible because the calf's head was turned backwards, the necessary fluids lost, and the uterus collapsed, entrapping and killing the youngster.

After a half hour's exhausting work with my face about one foot above a steaming drop filled with manure, I got a wire saw around the neck of the fetus and fed the wires back through a speculum. This instrument is no more than a fifteen inch piece of heavy white metal tubing, each end of which carried a rounded brass rim to protect delicate tissues. It was designed to be used in a cow's mouth to protect a stomach tube from razor sharp molars. I also found it useful in filling recessed gas tanks when I ran out of gas, protecting myself from frightened dogs doing their duty at some farms, disciplining spoiled horses, serving as a jack handle and spanner wrench extension, discouraging crime-minded hitch-hikers, and at the moment serving as a vaginal speculum.

As I worked, the labors of the mother were exhausting her and coming close to breaking my forearm. I clipped the hair at the end of her spine (or the beginning of her tail), inserted a needle between the vertebrae and deposited five cc's of local anesthetic in the space surrounding her spinal cord. The tired animal visibly relaxed as pain and abdominal press, in response to my manipulations, subsided.

"Mr. Assistant" stood behind me hurling invectives at the cow and I handed him the two handles that were then attached to each end of the wire saw. He was directed to seat himself behind me on the barn floor and start sawing with long deliberate strokes while I held the speculum in place to protect the cow.

"How come I ain't hurtin' her monkey?" my surgical assistant inquired as he saw the wire saw he wielded disappearing into the animal's vulva.

"Because I figured that one out ahead of time," I answered. I noticed as I looked at him that his purple lips were almost black and his breathing was labored. I pondered his own diagnosis for an instant and then asked him to change places with the owner who had just come upon the scene.

"From the looks of this I sure hope you know what you're doing, Doc!" he said.

As I regulated my answer to let him know that I had done this before and had not inadvertently placed the saw around the mother's heart, my second assistant fell backwards to roll on the grit on the barn floor with the entire saw in his hands.

"Wot da hell happened?" he managed to grunt from the reclining position I was chortling at.

"You cut off its head by utilizing this wire device at about the level of the sixth cervical vertebrae," I replied.

"Jeez!" he said.

I attached my chrome plated chains to the front legs of the calf and then engaging to the chain the same handles I had used on the wire saw, I handed one to each of my sensitive companions. With mild traction, during which my two companions felt fulfillment and satisfaction because they knew they would accomplish in five minutes what they had been trying to do all day, the headless calf was delivered. I then entered the mother with my arm up to my shoulder, retrieved the head and, standing with a flourish that said I wanted to be paid, deposited it at the feet of my silent employers.

"Gaud!" they said in unison.

I spanked the mother to her feet so that the uterus would not evert, and felt a rush of emotion in my throat and back of my eye-balls as she looked at me with quiet wonderment and then past me searching for her calf. Her only view at that instant was the two men dragging a headless calf down the steaming alley and with a subdued bellow she said good-bye to her child. I locked her stanchion and went to the feed cart to get her mind off the tragedy with some grain, and with a flicker in her eye her mind left the problem and she went to the constant reflex of eating. I knew that her calf was better dead than being sold the next day to "Da Joo" and packed in a cold truck with other unfortunates to be hauled about for hours and then slaughtered for veal. People who buy cattle at the farm, be they Black, Arab, or Irish are known by the New England farmers as "Da Joo". The owner returned.

"Too bad you couldn't save the calf, Doc." He was really oblivious to the fact that it was his fault and was thinking only of the sixteen to eighteen dollars he had lost by not being able to sell the calf.

"Well," I said, "based on prices last week at the auction, that cow is worth close to five hundred dollars!"

"Yep," he replied. "I'll send you a check when the milk check comes in."

Happy that he had gotten my message I said, "twenty-five will do plus six more for oxytocin and spinal anesthetic."

"Geez!" he breathed.

I got the check three weeks later with an enclosed note that the hired hand had been found dead in the barn, face down in the drop with a cow standing on his head. I was not upset by this.

I went into the milk room and washed up my instruments, made the decision about not changing coveralls, and sloshed my clammy way through the mud to my car. I turned out of the farm driveway and headed down the mountain.

My thoughts returned to a Sunday night when I came down this same hill ten years before in a borrowed car, driving to a

7

lacerated horse that the owner had pressured me about during the previous few hours. My son had just been operated on for appendicitis, the surgery unnecessarily delayed by doctors to fit their schedule. The delay caused a friable appendix that was broken on removal, with subsequent abcessation and considerable pain to my son. The tension had existed since Friday night and only respect for the doctors involved and pressures of trying to answer all the calls in the beginnings of a practice had halted me from blowing up at the surgeon. My son and been in pain and danger, endured mainly because of confidence in what his Dad told him, while the surgeon let things go until it was convenient to operate. I had taken into consideration other possible diagnoses, but they had passed by that time. I had blamed the tissue committee at the hospital for staying his hand because surgeons worked in constant fear of removing normal tissue. In the end I blamed lack of fortitude on the surgeon's part. When I realized my son's surgery was over and my son safe, there were unexpected tears of relief and sobs I never knew had piled within me as I drove down the mountain in the night long ago.

Be that as it may, I remembered the sense of being alone at last, answering the pleadings of a client under pressure by what he thought was a fatal laceration of his prize brood-mare.

The mare was calmly munching hay when I arrived, ignoring the square foot of bloody hide she had ripped from her shoulder. She was in no danger, but the owner, who was to become a valued client over the years, was on the verge of collapse. My work a great majority of the time is keeping in tune that pulsating, necessary, insidiously powerful bond of emotion that exists between mankind and his beloved animals. Granted that sometimes this bond is one of economics, it is more often one of love. The ability to shift from handling one emotion to the other in the course of a day and to be sensitive as to which bond exists, is one of the major things that makes a veterinarian of value to others and to his own sense of self.

Tonight, however, halfway down the mountain, I could see that my usual fast rate of speed was overtaking two cars in the mist ahead of me and in my mirror I saw two headlights come over the hill behind me traveling fast. There was a flicker of a shadow for an instant in the gleam of light below me on the road and instinct told me that something was amiss. I shifted the automatic gear down to bring my car a little more under control and drove on warily. In a few seconds my headlights reflected from the white under-belly of a deer that had been hit by the car ahead and for that instant was in a bizarre, disoriented pirouette of a dance of fear, her front legs clawing for the sky and her frantic eyes garishly reflecting my headlights. She had run from the quiet of the forest into the whirlwind of civilization, smashed with a force she never knew existed, and then came into full view of my lights. I watched carefully in that brief instant to see which way I would have to steer to avoid her and the slowing car that hit her. She righted herself and scrambled up a long pine-studded bank to the right as I steered quickly to the left.

This was all happening in just a few seconds and I was slowing to tell the stopped car ahead that all was well when an automatic glimpse in my mirror showed the car behind me rapidly bearing down. I instinctively accelerated and pulled out of danger not knowing if it was a drunk or a police officer. The siren and flashing lights gave me my answer as I leveled out at the bridge at the foot of the mountain. I slapped on my hazard lights, reached for my license and watched, after I halted, while an officer with a square shoulder adjusted his Sam Brown belt and with an upright swagger telling of his youth, came through the mist in the flashing lights of his cruiser. By the time he reached my car I had opened the window and had my license in hand. His voice started before his light came through my window. He had obviously missed the whole deer episode.

"Excuse me, Sir, but don't you think you were driving too fast down the mountain?....Jesus Christ!"

His light had just revealed the blood splashed coveralls and perhaps thinking he had just stumbled upon the goriest murder in a decade, his inexperienced face visibly blanched and his hand moved to the comfort of his holster.

"Yes, Sir. I was over the speed limit but I was cold and wet from delivering a calf and anxious to get to a hot shower," I said, trying to give him respite from shock as quickly as possible.

"Christ, Doc!" he exclaimed, recognizing my profession by what I said, by my uniform, and by my radio antenna. "Go ahead and get home, but please drive slower!"

"Thanks a lot," I replied. As I pulled away I saw his silhouette in his headlight, the shoulders not so square, since he had just absorbed one of many shocking episodes that he will have to on his way to becoming a member of a very valuable and elite corps of people .. the experienced State Troopers.

Good fortune smiled as I completed the next four miles to my house uneventfully. I settled the car in the garage and let out my beautiful dog who walked half asleep across my lap. She instinctively knew we were home and gave my face a slurp with her tongue as she went out the door. I sat for a moment with my head back feeling like a machine that had been shifted into neutral. My great cat was in the garage perched for its residual warmth on top of the crematory I used for animal disposal and his fang-laden mouth opened and closed with a greeting that would have been audible if the comfort of his heated perch had not taken away just enough energy to render him too lazy to produce a yowl to go with the oral activity. He knew that I knew what it meant, and besides, he was saving his strength for the occasional rat that he caught in order to produce an alibi for using my equipment for a pre-heated throne.

I walked from the garage across the asphalt reflecting how, in the past, I had come home so many times in the same way. In the early years, no garage, no blacktop; only mud, hope, and confidence. I remembered how my son and daughter had helped me build the retaining walls, fascinated by the cement mixer Daddy borrowed and shoveling .. three of sand by my son, one of cement by my daughter. Then the rush for the hose as I hauled the rocks. There is a lot of happiness in those walls and, thankfully, a warm memory of my children's eagerness to help and their confidence in their Dad. My wife helped me willingly in those days and handled

11

the phone, building client confidence in me as a veterinarian and learning so much about people. I thought how the situation had changed now, and I silently absorbed with appreciation my dog's tail-wagging warmth and affection as she walked, looking back over her shoulder to be sure I was coming toward the now almost darkened house.

The warmth of the clinic, under the house in those days, brought into focus the icy wetness that clung to my back and I peeled off the offensive coveralls, convinced that the surface of my liver must look like a frosted window in winter. I checked the stage of anesthesia on a few animals I had operated on that afternoon and headed for the shower.

When I entered my bedroom there was a muffled scream from under the pillows. As usual, my sleepy wife was certain that I was Jack the Ripper come to carve my name in her inviolable bosom.

"Oh! It's you," she said. "Hello, Honey....you must be cold....hurry to bed."

"I think I'll shower first."

"Lord!" she exclaimed. "You'd better!"

I had just passed her and the breath of my passing had wafted the previously mentioned aromatic mosaic to her delicate nostrils.

"Remember, Darling, as I told you fifteen years ago, that smells like bread and butter."

The answer was a practiced groan.

Undressing in the adjacent bathroom it flicked through my head that my wife's invitation to bed was, unfortunately, initiated by a maternal instinct, not a sexual one. I knew that in later years even this would be priceless.

The steaming hot water hit the back of my neck and coursed down my body with caressing warmth. My mind was tired, but my body waked to lecherous physical yearnings. Again my memory went back to another Sunday night past.

I was fifteen and, although six feet tall, a little over fat. I always tended to be alone when I could because things in which I was interested were then disturbed by my less sensitive cousins and friends. I found myself capably athletic and strong, and, as I remember, my main worry at that time was whether my pecker was big enough for the job for which it was intended. I was wandering around the hay barn on my Grandfather's estate hunting for woodchucks with a little twenty-two rifle that was my pride and joy. I had developed an animal sense by observation and could, by alternately walking and stopping, get very easily within range of these poor near-sighted rodents.

The sun was close to setting when I leaned against the barn, watching the valley below settle itself, like a brooding hen onto eggs, into nightfall. Somewhere above my head there was a giggle and I looked up to see two girls, one my age and tall and one very young and small, standing in the hay door. These girls had been visiting at the estate and I had spoken to them vaguely in the past weeks. The tall one was about fourteen, seemed to have a constant supply of shorts that were too tight and halters that were too loose. I had noticed a week before that she was, unknown to herself, in possession of an animal physical warmth, a very beautiful young and large bosom, and legs and bottom that moved in such a way as to disturb any male anywhere. In her eyes at this moment was a sparkling, taunting mischief that I or any of my farmer friends now would recognize as "bullin'" or " horsin'". This gal was in heat and I didn't know it then....nor did she.

"Hi!"' I said looking up, and just as quickly down when my gaze just happened to go up one pant leg. The low angled sunlight had revealed one half of her crotch and I was pole-axed!"

"Betcha can't guess what we're doing," she practically sang.

"Nope," I managed to gurgle. "What's up?" I said that into the side of the barn. I couldn't look up again and stay mentally with it. This I knew.

"We made a hay slide and it goes all the way to the barn floor from here," she sang. "It's fun and it feels good when you slide on your tummy and we always end up in a big tangled pile at the bottom. Wanna try?"

I think there was a sound that came from my mouth as I struggled with the cacophony of feelings inside of me. I wanted to go badly, but wasn't sure I knew what to do when I got there. She wanted more than a hay-slide, but I didn't know how I knew. The little girl whose eyes shone from the previous "play" went down the slide first and quickly got aside on the barn floor and I followed feet first. I had just about arrived at the hay covered barn floor when the laughing big girl that followed slid into place

14

close beside me and as I cleared my face of the hay that had accompanied her, my first sight was the open-mouth-silent-fascinated gaze of the ten year old girl standing to the side and above me. I turned my head to see about the big girl and immediately in front of my eye was the upright pink nipple of her young breast that had been slipped from beneath her halter in the slide. By instinct my lips went to it immediately, and my hand went between her legs where her shorts had been forced aside in the slide. She groaned and writhed against me, reached out and caressed between my legs all in the space of about eight seconds, and I, with my one uncovered eye staring into the wholly entranced face of the other girl, had the fastest orgasm in history without even the distinction of an erection. Bells, bulbs, and bombs burst within my body and mind as I rushed from the barn into the summer fields with their fireflies, wild-flowers, and vibrant sounds and smells of evening. An hour's time alone in the fields and then I stole into the house and crept secretly to bed. The rumpled night that followed gave birth to many notions about morality, and in addition to that, jelled all the facts that I had gleaned from other boys concerning masturbation - the young animal's safety valve.

Confusion reigned a week later when I asked the girl to come to the hay barn and she tossed her head and walked away looking as if I had just spit on her lapel. The mental and physical cycle with which I was to become so familiar in females of many species was manifest and the girl was acting normally instead of pretending to hide behind a "mystique" that she liked to believe she invented.

"Humans are the only animal that can be talked into heat," a professor of veterinary medicine was to say many years later and sometimes a busy, involved man has little time to talk. The woman who instinctively and inventively makes him provide the time automatically is the woman who he will love.

These thoughts again had barely flitted through my mind as I showered and I stepped from the sequestered little stall where no one could reach me. I was warm, clean, and charged with wanting a woman. I slipped beneath the sheets and reached for the soft, sculptured hips of my sleepy wife. She turned and patted my shoulder as you would burp a child. I rolled on my back and smiled at the depth of passion that twenty years of marriage produce in a woman and grimaced, knowing her lack of aggression, even though she was rested, was partly my fault. Sleep came rapidly after I set the alarm at six-thirty noticing the time was then eleven P.M.

The phone's first piercing scream came five minutes later constricting my cardiac vessels and sending my pulse into my ears. Thinking that I would have to stop being so concerned or someday face myocardial infarction, I managed a bright "Hello!"

"Oh, hello, Doctor," an elderly voice said. "I knew you would be looking at the Sunday night movie so I waited until now to call. I tried earlier but your machine said you were out. I do hope you had a good day off but I wanted to talk a bit about my little Tigger".

It was Mrs. Hyphen. I could never remember her hyphenated last name so I always mentally referred to her as Mrs. Hyphen. As I struggled to gain some composure and tried sleepily to remember what part of her anatomy a little tigger was, it dawned on me that she was referring to her little poodle that I had operated on two weeks earlier. I considered telling her that I didn't have a day off and instructing her not to hang up on the answering machine, but to listen for telephone numbers where I could be reached so that late calls could be avoided, but I knew it would be wasted effort. She wouldn't be listening.

"What seems to be the trouble?" I asked, using a really original phrase.

"It seems to me that Tigger is bothered somewhat by the surgery you did. He just is not himself psychologically and doesn't behave himself around the house," Mrs. Hyphen explained in a secretive tone.

Well, this meant to me that horny old "Tigger", whom I had castrated earlier because of a vastly enlarged prostate at age twelve, either was lifting his leg all around the house or was trying to screw every cat in his immaculately appointed home. Either could be a symptom of urethritis from the prostate.

"What's he doing, Ma'm?"

"He is somewhat depressed and is aaah, wetting around the house. You know he never had any - uh - contact with females in his life. Do you suppose I could have saved him this suffering if I had allowed him to - aah - take on a little girl dog?" the voice asked in a subdued tone.

17

"No," I exclaimed, "I think I know what's wrong. Would you send him in at office hours at two o'clock tomorrow, please?"

I felt like saying that even a normal dog is in luck these civilized days if he gets more than one or two pieces of tail in a year--and then he may get half his ass chewed off by the competition during the act. I decided this realistic thought was not for the likes of her and awaited her answer.

"Will he be all right tonight, Doctor?" the voice asked concernedly.

"Give him a half teaspoon of the good Courvoisier you have," I said with some misgivings as it is not too good for urethritis, but, as I had figured, the answer was good for her.

Mrs. Hyphen breathed a grateful "Thank you, Doctor, and goodnight," and then rushed off to play nurse and have a little nip with sexy old Tigger.

My wife stirred beside me and mumbled sleepily, "Mrs. T. called to inquire about old Socrates and was upset because you hadn't called."

Old Socrates was a wonderful black cat that had been admitted two days earlier for a urethral blockage so common in castrated male cats. I had cared for the animal since it was a kitten and we knew and liked each other very well. I had checked him when I dumped my coveralls in the tub and could see the urine was still flowing freely though there was no voluntary control after the catheter was removed. The look in Old Soc's eyes pleaded with me to give him something for the extreme discomfort, and I had popped a pill down his throat in passing. During the

18

course of the day I had, on two occasions, because I had a few minutes free, tried to call Mrs. T. but received no answer. I was concerned because I knew her and she would be worried about old Soc. How could she know that Soc was not my only case that day or that I was as fond of him as she? She had called because she was certain, after seventy-some years of inexperience, that since I had not called I certainly didn't care.

A general practice exposes a man to calls at all times of the day or night. At this hour no farmers would call because they work hard and need their sleep. Tragedy from them is reported at five in the morning when they walk into the barn and find it. Telephone calls from owners of dogs and cats don't start until nine in the morning when they are getting up and around, but they are liable to continue into late evening as they sit watching the mind-bending TV set.

I breathed a prayer that all was well in the animal world of my "parish" and fell back on the pillow, sleeping before I hit it.

****

CHAPTER TWO: Monday morning

The phone had jangled at 5:30 AM and an anxious voice had said, "Doc, can you come right away? June is down and bloated and it don't look like milk fever!"

Here was a different man then the one I had delivered the calf for the night before, and my compassion was immediately triggered for him as well as his beautiful cow named June, an animal capable of producing over one hundred pounds of milk daily but who had to be handled like a delicate watch with respect to feeding and management.

"I'll be there, Antonio," I said. "Try to brace up her rear quarters and be sure she has a bale to lean her side against."

"Okay," he said with relief in his voice and hung up hurriedly so that he could proceed with the daily routine of milking, cleaning, and feeding fifty head of Holstein cattle, plus heifers and calves. I knew that now he was relieved of a burden of responsibility and I was shouldering that load for a time because that is what my life was all about and I savored the challenge. For a while I was to be a vital force in the life of another man, possibly holding the destiny of an animal we both loved in my hands, trying to avoid the economic loss of a producing cow, and juggling the emotions of an emergency situation not only to make it bearable if we lost but also to keep the participants efficient enough to help us all towards a possible triumph. This situation was to be repeated often throughout the day, the week, the year, and my life.

When I hung up the phone my warm wife had stirred beside me.

"Oh, Honey," she said. "I'm sorry you have to go. You must be tired and it's cold out."

A wife can do no more than that and I appreciated it to the point where I reached over and patted her bare bottom with thanks. Being a morning person as far as peak efficiency is concerned, I also added a lecherous pinch in the right place which produced a snort and a pillow pulled over her head. I got up rapidly and dressed.

I had learned a while back not to rush headlong to a call like this, but to prepare and think while I started my car to warm it up. I returned to the house to let out my happy full bladdered dog and to warm myself with hot chocolate.

The bland cold light of a late winter dawn silhouetted the stark hardwood trees on the hills behind my house, and I paused for a moment beside my car and listened. My dog had come out of the dark to stand beside me as we heard the sounds of coming Spring. Tiny creeks that exist for a while this time of year, plus more permanent streams, all hurried gaily down the almost frozen hillsides and rushed to join the big river in the valley and they all joined to produce the dull roar of an awakening world that no one hears unless he is up and attentive at this hour. I entered the car behind my setter, faced the familiar smells and drove down

21

the valley through patches of mist, feeling very much alive, very useful, and very pleased with my burdens.

The drive was quiet. I felt I had much company from the lights of various farms and from the houses of people I knew to be early risers. I noted with pleasure the newly active coons as they scurried across the road in my lights. The day before I had seen a few dead by the roadside, and though sad about their demise, their activity announced Spring as did the frantic flying and screaming of the crows approaching their breeding time and as did the arrival in the sky of the black vultures soaring in the uncertain spring air currents.

Antonio's barn was warm, clean, and well lighted when I arrived and the sounds of the cattle eating, the calves bawling softly, and the synchronous tic tic of the milking machine signified a well run dairy. I examined June quickly and told Antonio to time his milking so that he could help me in about ten minutes.

I assured myself that the udder was not gangrenous and checked her slow steady pulse.

Antonio said, "She had a fine big bull calf yesterday morning but I helped her because it was backwards!"

My mind clicked immediately to examine for a second calf because more often than not a twin born first is presented backwards. The cow herself had a light wobble to her gaze as she turned to look at me and the sluggish response of her pupil to my flashlight plus the clammy coldness of her extremities yielded the diagnosis of "milk fever". This condition is not a fever at all

22

but an inability of the parathyroid gland to mobilize calcium fast enough from bone and food to the blood stream at the time of acute milk production, i.e., birth. The first result of this low blood calcium is inability of the involuntary muscles, those over which an animal has no control such as uterus, intestine, and iris muscles to operate. Hence the calf had remained in the uterus and labor had waned. Obviously the treatment is to put calcium in the blood stream and I was about to get up to do this when I noticed a "cat nest" in the straw near June's foreleg. A mother cat was nursing five young kittens and stared at me with loud purring and squinty-eyed affection and trust. I picked up one kitten because I knew the mother trusted me and held it up in the early light from the barn window. I do this often in barns and am always drenched in wonder and vibrated with a feeling of protective affection that almost brings tears to my eyes as I look at the tiny furry beast staring back at me with tiny droplets of milk on its lips. These little inhabitants of every barn can usually look forward to a violent death crushed beneath some cow or a tractor, pierced by a pitchfork, or wound up in a machine belt. Their world in the barn is filled with wondrous dark alleys filled with interesting rodents and warm, cozy, hay-filled places to sleep in shafts of sunlight.

I heated a bottle of calcium solution in the milk room where I enjoyed the company of Antonio's daughter as she prepared nipple pails of milk to feed the calves. She was a buxom girl of seventeen, and, trusting me, she always tried out her feminine type of charm on me before applying it to the boys at school. In the sink my pail was filling with hot water over the medicine bottle as I held my hands in the welcome warmth and the girl passed behind me crowded somewhat by the milk tank. Her ample breasts brushed by back, moved back and forth and then remained warmly in place.

"Good morning, Crystal! You certainly are feeling well this morning."

"And so are you," she replied without moving but looking around my shoulder.

Her eyes held a mischievous sensuous glint and I gently lifted the pail and headed for the barn proper. I knew I would see her again and I honestly wanted to help June, not Crystal.

In a few minutes I had the nose lead in June and tied to her rear leg. This position presents the jugular vein for easy access. I inserted a needle, attached the bottle with rubber tubing and handed it to Antonio who had timed his milking to perfection in order to help. This was a man who moved efficiently, observed in a sensitive compassionate way, and knew his really important position in the world. He was what I called an "animal person" who sees and feels what is going on around him from minute to minute and can care for people as well as animals because he knows what forces make them tick. In a flicker my mind thought how closely we thought alike about the world, how inconspicuous was the existence of animal people and how well they communicated with each other; how we each used compassion as a tool knowing its depth and its value. Using it not necessarily when it was triggered within us but withholding it when dependence on it would create a cry for more, and minimizing it when it would create character.

24

Compassion held back is a powerful force to be used when it will create strength through love and security in true tragedy.

On the other hand I was glad this strong Lithuanian was not observant enough to have seen the episode in the milk room. My pulse and the butter-flies in my lower abdomen were just beginning to subside. Young as she was, Crystal's impact was to remain with me for years.

I scratched a barn cat's presented ear as I watched reflexes return in the glossy bovine form before me. Her skeletal muscles began to quiver, at last responding to the calcium. The sign I watched for, rhythmic though almost imperceptive abdominal contractions, began. Antonio was not far behind me in observing.

"You're right, Doc. She has another calf in there," he said.

"Well, let's get it out," I said as I headed for the wash bucket. "You had better hope it's a bull, Tony", I said. "It will be worth more to sell than a heifer and I guess you know you probably can't keep a heifer."

"Yep," he grunted. "What makes a 'freemartin' anyway, Doc?"

"Freemartin" is a name for an intersex individual that is common in bovines if it is a female born twin with a male.

"Well, Tony, when the two individuals are occupying the same uterus there often is a blending together of the circulation. The word is anastomosis, or connection of vessels. The male fetus usually is developing ahead of the female and at a critical time in growth of the embryo, the male hormones have an adverse affect on

25

the developing female and produce an intersex," I explained though I didn't believe science was positive of it.

As the big farmer held the bottle I examined the calf I had delivered easily as I talked and found that it was a "freemartin".

"You're selling this one, Tony," I said.

"How come you know so quick?" he asked with interest.

I pointed out that the calf had an extremely prominent clitoris, was certainly sterile and of no use as a herd addition.

"Well, damn me," Tony blurted. "A girl with a pecker!"

I smiled at the floor and noticed that the bottle Tony was holding was empty and he was about to fill June's blood vessels with possibly fatal air. I pinched the tube, pulled the needle from her vein and released the nose lead because I saw her apprehensive look at the squirming wet calf behind her. We carried the baby up front of the stanchion and when the big animal saw that we had left it just out of reach she jumped to her feet as we had hoped, threatened us with flopping ears, and proceeded to lick her baby.

"That's an awful good cow," said Tony. "Are you sure I can't raise that calf?"

"I'm sure," I answered. "Some need examination with a small speculum but this one doesn't. Some even have to be raised until rectal examination is possible but I'm sure of this one already. Sorry!"

"Okay. Say, while you're here could you examine some cows for pregnancy for me?"

"Not now, Tony. There are others holding cows in for me."

26

"You're right, Doc. I'll call you tonight.

As I packed my bag and Tony went back to work I watched the coming dawn through the frosty barn windows. High in the meadow across the creek four deer in a group picked their way to the hardwoods, browsing as they went. Their movements were unhurried because they knew Spring was not far away and food would be plentiful. The threat of dog packs running on crusted snow now was gone, and this was the month the fawns would start to arrive, first deep in honeysuckle thickets and later on at the edges of freshly sprouted alfalfa and clover fields. In the birch copse by the creek I spotted the swift low flight of a hunting hawk as he searched for his prey. I knew this to be a Coopers Hawk because of his size and method of hunting about thirty feet off the ground and wondered how many harmless soaring hawks were shot each year by uninformed marksmen who did not know that the real predators hunted swiftly just under tree level with not a sound.

I was filled at that moment with the happiness that comes only to a man who knows deep within himself that he is doing exactly what he was born to do and who had started that day, at least, with a triumph. Each day of my life I have striven for some small triumph even if it's known only to myself. To save the life of a trusting dog, to ease one out of life with a kind needle when his suffering is irreparable, to capture a known individual brown trout with a two pound gossamer leader and a number fourteen nymph, to calm a frightened colt into confidence, or to make a difficult shot on a familiar ruffed grouse as he explodes from in front of my hard working dog.

27

These are the little accomplishments that keep my face in the sun and remind me I am a man-animal walking the face of an accidentally beautiful planet fulfilling a function of value to others and dominating little problems, not other man-animals.

A warm hand closed on the exposed biceps of my right arm, as I stood, and I turned to look at Crystal's face. She had waited until her Dad had gone to another part of the barn and brought me a little kitten she wanted me to look at.

"The kitten's back is broken," I said as I examined it gingerly.

"I was afraid so. It was stepped on two days ago and I wouldn't let Daddy shoot it," she said with her clear brown eyes brimming with unloosened tears. "Would you put it to sleep for me?"

I gently injected some barbiturates that I carry for just this purpose and Crystal lay the little furry body on a hay bale at our feet.

Thank-you," Crystal said as she leaned over it supporting herself with one strong arm and gently stroking the kitten with the other hand. I put my hand on her shoulder and drop by drop Crystal's silent tears fell upon the kitten's fur reflecting the lights in the barn and the new sunlight of the day.

This sad vignette was over quickly, as this was a farm girl and used to the come and go of animal life. I picked up my bag, placed it in the car and looked up in response to a whispered, "Doc" that came from the barn window a few feet away. Crystal's lips were pursed as she motioned me a kiss and said quietly, "You're a big man, Doctor. Someday I really want to thank you!"

As I drove away sunlight and fires burst within me; my forty year old ego soared, and I gave unspoken thanks for those fleeting instants when suddenly young girls consider older men as men and not just father images.

The sun was on the rim of the hills now and I drove rapidly north up the mist laden valley, hungry and thinking of the day ahead, or at least thinking of the things I *knew* I had to do and hoping not too many calls would come in to explode a tight schedule. At nine I had a herd to check for pregnancy and breeding preparations. At ten-thirty a herd to test for TB. I had told Mrs. Alton-Smyth I would examine two mares for pregnancy about ten fifteen as her farm lay between the two previously mentioned. She had been given the mares and wanted to make sure the one was pregnant that was supposed to be. At twelve-fifteen I had a meeting at Mrs. Meany's with the health officer, the building inspector, the state dog warden, the ASPCA representative, and the assistant state dog warden to try and close down a so called "kennel" that I had tolerated long enough. At two o'clock normal office hours would start, after which I would do some surgery and work at my desk with my secretary. At four-thirty I had a date to worm two yearling quarter horse colts. All other calls that occurred would have to get into this schedule somehow.

I knew the time to be about seven-twenty because as I cruised rapidly up the valley I passed groups of high school students waiting in the cold for the long bus trip to the high

29

school twenty miles to the north. For ten miles I drove rapidly and each group waved with fond recognition, smiling and whooping and warming my every blood cell with their friendship. For a few years I had been chairman of the school board and I gave silent thanks for those that had joined me at that time to prevent the district from sending little seventh graders through this trip to the high school. Most of the people who advocated this change had never been on the roads in a winter dawn and knew nothing of the hardship involved for little children.

The bus coming towards me stopped beneath its flashing signals and I began to slow down preparatory to stopping. I would be directly in front of the bus going in the opposite direction, and I looked forward to seeing a friendly face at the wheel as I knew most of the drivers; but no..lo and behold there behind the wheel was the stern face of a large sized woman. I had seen the lady drivers in other towns and can practically never find a friendly face among them. They watch my every move knowing full well, I'm sure, that since they were carrying children, there has got to be some holy light about them and I dare not lift a finger from the righteous path that they had recently been taught I should adhere to. White knuckles tensely gripping large steering wheels tell tales of the rumbling bigger tension within. With set lips and a practiced frown these denizens of the coffee klatches go rigidly about their new jobs glaring down from their new found orange heights at the mere men below.

I looked at this one between acknowledging the yells of "hi ya, Doc" from the kids, and thought surely that coiling through her machine-like mind there had to be an oath that all the lady bus-drivers repeated in unison at lady-bus-driver school. Dedicated, filled with fear, admirable, but far from human, she sat above me as I thought of some way I could penetrate this cold steel wall and smile hello. I moved my car about six inches and instantly the eyes came down like a pointer on a quail and as lady-dreadnought screwed up scowl number one A (page 32b in manual). I winked hornily and waved. No good..her horn-rimmed glasses ablaze in the morning sunlight she turned her head to stare straight ahead and carefully put her vehicle in gear (page 31 in manual) and slowly started off. As she passed high above me, my left hand being on the top of my steering wheel, I raised the center finger for a fleeting triumphant second, and as I smoothly glided away I heard and saw that this mover of the masses indeed had fantastic peripheral vision. The gears screamed as she forgot the clutch timing and the vehicle wobbled at ten miles per hour as she searched the mirror. As was my intent, she was not actually certain that she had seen this respected professional citizen part with an obscene gesture. I was very happy!

"KJW425 calling car," blurted from beneath my dashboard and almost spun my setter off the seat as she awoke recognizing the voice of my wife.

I jerked the microphone up from its hook and said, "Good morning, Baby. What's up?" knowing she was standing in just arisen disarray in the kitchen.

"Newt Billson has a cow that calved three days ago and hasn't cleaned yet," she said tersely.

Me darlin' black haired colleen is not at her sweetest in the morning but she had taken the call and gotten it to me fast as I had always asked, even though her schedule was interrupted. Also Newt had called early as I always asked, and the combination was working well because Newt's place was five minutes from where I was.

"Thanks, Darling. I'll get that done right now," I replied.

"You eat breakfast," mother-wife said over the airways.

"Keerect," I answered as I wheeled the big car into a right turn up the hillside to the Billson farm and in three minutes turned into the barnyard as Newt came out of the barn.

"Jesus Christ, Doc. You must be short of cash this month. I never had such service," Newt blurted with a sparkle in his eye. "I was just headed for breakfast. That cow can wait half an hour. C'mon up to the house and the old lady will feed ya'".

In earlier years when I opened practice I would have said, "No thanks. Just show me the cow and I'll take care of her while you eat."

Now I knew that the nucleus of living and enjoying was to take these instants - when proud, hard working people wanted you for an extemporaneous guest - and wring from them all the experience and observation I could get. In the previous ten years I had known this man as we struggled in a mosquito swamp to save a down cow, as we delivered a calf on a sun-lit ridge in summer, as we examined cows and discussed world politics in a quiet barn. We spoke also of lecherous experiences, the raising of children, and new farm trends and equipment. I know many men like this

32

along with their wives and the clean simple kitchens in which they live, and so it was here; the best coffee and eggs that one could imagine, and we returned to the barn to my patient.

A blind man could find the animal with a retained placenta. The odor is powerful. As I washed the cow with disinfectant soap I could read Newt's thoughts as he held the tail to the side and gurgled slightly behind a greenish white face.

"Better hang on to that great breakfast," I said as my plastic covered arm plunged deep into the inflamed uterus. Thinking I would give him something else to think about I said what I thought was an original saying. "That's enough to gag a maggot," hoping to make him laugh.

"Gawd!" he squealed. "That ud chase a dog off a gut-wagon."

Completely topped, I shut up and removed the placenta, admiring once again the delicate membrane that gives life and nutrition to the young growing fetus.

"How come they stick sometimes?" he asked.

I explained how the placenta fits into the uterus as two hair brushes would go together and that swelling, caused either by infection or trauma or both, would cause retention.

I inserted some soluble antibacterial tablets. "Be sure I see her on the next routine herd check," I said.

"Okay! I'll call in about two weeks before plowing starts."

Cleaned up and with a change of coveralls I felt great, but a check of the car clock said I had better keep moving. The time was 8:40, and I had eighteen miles to the herd I had to check for pregnancy and infertility The man would be impatiently waiting to turn out 120 head of cattle in order to start cleaning the barn. The longer they stayed in because of me the fuller the barn became. I gunned the big motor and called my wife by radio.

"KJW425.."

"Yes, Honey," Patience replied.

"Will you ask Boss-Lady to check by radio when she takes over? There are two patients I want to know about and a few surgical cases coming in I want *her* to know about."

"Can do."

"I'm headed for Fallon's on the mountain," I said.

"Right."

I reflected on the romantic nature of our conversation after twenty years of marriage. Continuing reflection of the past, I let my mind go back thirty years or so to a Monday morning that found me poised on a long chicken coop roof. I was watching as my grandfather's great thoroughbred gelding grazed closer and I prepared to leap upon his back and ride with the wind. At that time I was not familiar with the nature of hot-blooded horses, but I was killing time at the farm because the day before Thin Jim had said the animal doctor was coming. I had asked for what purpose and got a grunt for an answer. This I knew immediately had to do with sex because Thin Jim never talked about that. Thin Jim was a tall man with leather skin, an aquiline face, and a great mustache. He was general caretaker for my grandfather and I dogged the footsteps of his bony, sinewy frame every summer. He was very careful of his conversation with me concerning the earthier

34

aspects of raising animals except for one time when I asked him why he kept the cow separate after the "Jew" had brought the young bull in his filthy truck for a brief physical encounter with one of our cows that I noticed had been bawling more then the others.

"Well," Jim explained as his embarrassment was punctuated by magnificent squirts of tobacco juice, "when she was bullin' three weeks ago she got so springy ridin' them other cows I figger she lost what the bull put in so she didn't get caught."

From that one sentence that was carefully spoken in a voice that had become familiar, I, as a young boy, began a long journey from the depths of ignorance. I had learned that the bull's performance had left something within the cow and also that females are apt to do this thing in cycles.

At present, however, the horse was now directly beneath me and unconscious of my presence. This, I thought, was an advantage mainly because I didn't know horses very well. I feared them greatly and wanted very much to conquer that fear. To be brief, I launched myself from the coop to a position on the great back and grabbed a handful of mane. The kind horse launched me once more into the morning sun describing an arc that ended in the run-off from the manure pit. I remember now looking up through buzzing flies, American pokeweed leaves, and a stench so strong it was almost visible, to see the quizzical face of the monster horse staring down at me from the hillock into which the cement manure pit was built. In those days I was sure he was sure he was going to stomp me into the muck to become a fossil. Now I know he was only wondering what I was and from where had I come. At that moment the animal doctor arrived.

I heard his car and saw a cloud of dust come around the barn as he stopped. I walked into the back of the barn as he and Thin Jim walked in the front talking.

"My God, Boy!" Dr. Fred said. "Whatcha been doing?"

"I fell," I barked, and walked on by, headed for the watering trough.

"Wow!" Jim said as I walked by. "I think you died a week ago."

There have been many times when I have thought the most refreshing place in the world was a spring-fed watering trough, but at that moment, as I stared into its green-mossy depths filled with life forms I knew nothing about then, I was sure there was no place I needed more. I jumped right in, washed and returned to the barn in time to see the Dr. behind a cow with his arm inserted into her rectum up to his shoulder.

I was not shocked. I was thoroughly intrigued, specially when he said to Jim, "She'll be around earlier that you expect. Look for her in heat next week."

"Should I breed her?" queried Jim.

By God! I thought. You can control this cycle thing. I went outside as they talked and looked over the Vet's car. It was new and packed with bottles, instruments, tubes, a pail, and smells. The doctor came out then into the sun in front of the barn rolling up his great rubber sleeve. He put a strong brown hand on my shoulder.

36

"Son, you sure look and smell better. Better luck next time. So long."

He was in his car and going down the gravel road. I stood in the settling dust and thought that here was a man that kept moving, kept in good shape, a prisoner of neither desk nor boss, and lifelong investigator of all the puzzles of animal life I had been seeing in the world around me. At that moment, one that I can remember as vividly as this morning, I knew I would become a veterinarian. During the war I ignored it because of more urgent matters but I never changed. There was tremendous strength in having this knowledge.

"KJW425!!!!!!!!, calling car," the powerful voice of Boss-Lady came from the radio speaker like a truck hitting a great Chinese gong. This time my setter leapt and struck her head on the panel as I struggled to control the car now influenced by the reverberations of my ear drum. I calmed myself by wondering why I used a radio with the out-put Boss-Lady had and how I could possibly harness all that power to my own advantage.

"Car, over," I replied quietly.

"HELLO, YOU OLD GOAT," she said. My calm, quiet nurse let me know that it was Monday morning and she was feeling great after four days off. This lady was in her early fifties, ruddy of skin with brilliant eyes and bushy uncontrollable hair, and was built like a wrestler. She possessed unfaltering strength, and an opinionated almost unmalleable mind, and (though she didn't know it) an eighth sense about animal nature. I'm sure her blocky frame was taken up almost entirely by heart. This woman who

37

spoke her mind, reasoned like a child and used childlike ploys to gain attention, kept my clinic spotlessly clean, dogged my heels by radio, phone, or in person until the last animal under her care got my attention. She was now checking in as I had asked, rested from days off and really oblivious that everyone else had been working. Boss-Lady was determined to take over her leadership by means of writing notes, giving me hell for leaving a dirty syringe over the weekend or throwing all items she didn't understand from the surgery/examining room onto my uncluttered business desk and daring me silently to challenge her authority to do so. I had learned to ignore the silent challenge and give her some other thing to think about.

"I think the white terrier has pyometra," I said. "I'm waiting for the WBC from the lab, but I am sure of it anyway. Surgery will require constant IVs. The tiger cat must have that eye out today without fail!"

"My God, Doc. You have two spays coming in that I know about, and two x-rays to take. How will we get it all done?" she crackled as her well organized day began to fall apart.

"I don't know but I'll cross that bridge at two o'clock. Right now I have work to do out here and I have to leave the clinic by four thirty to worm some horses," I threw at her. "Just be sure to be ready."

She depressed the transmission button purposely so I could hear her groan, "Oh, my Gawd!"

"I'm headed for Fallon's on the mountain. The number is in the file and call in any calls on the road so I can try and keep ahead of things," I requested.

"What if you don't answer the radio?" she asked petulantly.

"Try again in ten minutes," I ordered.

She tended to forget that her occasional ten yard walk to the radio could save me many miles on the road and sometimes hours of going back over ground covered in the morning.

"Okay, Doc," she said as she confidently settled down to work.

Almost all animals respond to discipline and show confidence and ability under it, whereas they are insecure and downright dangerous in an atmosphere of permissiveness. It matters not if this atmosphere is created by design, by ignorance, or by giving the action the name of "love" or "compassion". The end result is the same. Behind every aggressive German Shepherd or "hard to handle" horse you will find a hesitant, timorous, non-animal person and I believe so it goes with children. The boundaries must be set firmly, for they will constantly make sorties to find them, and during these sorties they are "rotten kids".

The clock on the dash read 9:10 as I wheeled past the lake on the mountain at Fallon's farm and noted, with a warm feeling, that the geese were on the lake on their way north. They were feeling well and a little sexy because, though they weren't feeding, there was activity and game playing in the cove with much wing-beating and apparent stretching. The length of their journey the day before would suggest they'd want rest, but the longer hours of sunlight were having an effect on their physical activity. The stirrings of sexual awakenings gave strength to their bodies.

I stopped the big car beside a smaller shed with a southeast exposure where the minor population of the farm, dogs and cats, now slept in the morning sun. I always take time to greet these rural citizens, and I usually stop where they are because they know the most comfortable places to loaf. Here was such a place: On the window sills and in the angle between the weather-worn wood and the warm moist ground green shoots of oats and grasses growing in new splendor from seeds blown there in the fall. The wood stored the warmth of the sun and at night the frost did not kill so here was the first place that became a living world in the Spring. Every farm has a place like this. They are easy to find if you look for the resting cats and dogs. Or me!

No men were in sight so I made my way down the drive to where I had seen someone moving through the kitchen window. I entered the warm kitchen and sitting on a chair by the stove, her legs braced and supporting herself by one arm on the stove, sat thirty-five-year-old Mrs. Fallon with a look on her face that combined horror with futility.

"Can I help you with anything, Cathy?" I asked. "What's wrong?"

She gurgle-sighed and motioned with her thumb to the back door. I strode quickly over and quietly opened the door to look out in the sun lit back yard. It took a moment to take in the scene but finally I shuddered with horror and closed the door quietly to think. In the back yard were two young boys, the Fallons, one six, one nine, dressed in cowboy suits sitting on boxes and drinking water out of coke bottles. On their hips were six-guns and they lounged man fashion with their feet up on boxes as they solemnly gazed upon the gently swinging furry bodies of three kittens they had just lynched with baling twine. I leaned my forehead against the door frame as I cursed television and the movies for their blatant lack of taste and common sense in appealing to the barbarism in all of us. I walked out and cut down the little animal forms. I towered above the kids and spoke firmly.

"I am as big to you as you were to the kittens. I could hang you easily as you did the babies - *think about it!*"

I hoped I commanded the respect and strong memories as did the sight of my first veterinarian

Since I didn't know what to say to Cathy Fallon I went to the barn to get on with my work. "Bo" Fallon had the list ready, and I had about forty head to examine. Under contemporary farm economy, a cow must be re-bred and pregnant again within one hundred days after calving. If she isn't, she will lose money the following year during a prolonged "dry" period during which she eats but gives nothing in return because the birth of a new calf is delayed. It's a great challenge because I must recognize infection, hormone imbalances, and anatomical derangements, and correct them before the critical one hundred days are up. I like the challenge and enjoy the work.

Of the forty head I was to examine some were early pregnancy exams that I diagnose rectally by feeling for gossamer like membranes in the uterus forty days after breeding, but most were so called "fresh" cows that had calved and I must prepare for re-breeding.

Some I had stimulated to come in heat again by ovarian manipulations, and I had infused bacteria killing agents through plastic catheters into the genital tracts of others.

I finished working in about an hour. We were walking towards the car when Bo said, "There is a cow here, chain number 37, that is supposed to be pregnant but doesn't look it. Think you ought to look at her?"

Since I knew the man to be observant I agreed, and rectal examination revealed a problem.

"This cow's carrying a mummy calf, Bo. What's her production record?"

"Goddamn!" said Mr. Fallon. "She's a top cow!"

A mummy calf is a calf that dies at about three months of age but is not expelled. The membranes dry up and it has a mummy-like appearance. I could remove it from this cow with drugs but again that would prolong that nonproductive period, and whether to keep her or salvage her for beef at beef prices would be dictated by her potential production when she finally calved again. For this information Mr. Fallon consulted the IBM sheet that showed her last production and profit over feed cost.

"She gave eighteen thousand pounds last year," Bo said.

"No question. Abort her and we will breed her again," I said.

"I guess we should try, Doc."

I injected a large dose of a specific hormone and headed quickly for my car so that I could still make the interim stop at Mrs. Alton-Smyth's before getting to the herd tuberculin testing down the road.

The waning snow tread tires, my third set that winter, spewed a mixture of mud and manure from the mushy barnyard in a satisfying arc. The dogs rose quickly from their places in the sun to manifest their territorial rights by chasing me from the farm and as I turned onto the mountain road, two minuscule cowpunchers emptied their six-guns at me from behind a hedge. I believe a man could make a fortune if he found a market for kittens and baling twine, but never want to see them get together again like that.

I stopped down the road for a moment to write out charge slips for the calls so far and to check in to the office while the topography lent itself to good radio communications. I noted the time to be ten twenty.

"Wha'd'ya want, Doc?" said Boss-Lady, disgruntled. I had obviously disturbed her routine as had phone calls and people driving in before my call. She was sometimes difficult to convince that I was the boss and even more difficult to convince that clients were necessary things and sometimes a lot more troubled than she.

"I am headed for Mrs. Alton-Smyth's to do those pregnancy exams on the mares she was given," I explained. "Have any other troubles developed?"

"The white doggie is throwing up and Mr. Stonecold called to be sure you would be there to test his cows on time. The little boy who owns the tiger cat with its eye knocked out called and asked you to save the eyeball for him when you remove it. Some others called but I told them to call back or come in at two o'clock. I have to leave here at one o'clock sharp to get my check in the bank so you be in to sign!" she squalled.

"We will fix the terrier, I'll get to Stonecold almost on time, have a jar of formalin ready for that eye-ball, and forget about your bank deadline. If they jail you I'll get you out!" I replied.

Her reply came back steeped in menopausal adrenalin. I quickly turned down the volume and headed my car through the hardwood-lined mountain top road. I knew then I would be about one half hour late for Mr. Stonecold. If there were any other delays I would be late for that great gathering of officials I had precipitated to close Mrs. Meany's terrible kennel.

The road bend ahead suddenly revealed the unmistakable strut of a ruffed grouse as he patrolled his territory. Approaching Spring gets to all the animals and at this time of year a grouse will go out of his way to attack intruders around his domain. I went around him and started to slow to a stop as I often will wait for these birds to gain the brush and then give my dog a little practice on finding the wind and holding a point. I had passed and my mirror revealed the bird actually in the air attacking my rear window. He soon dropped to a hillock among some laurel beside the road and stood with full neck ruff and fan tail. I let my dog out the opposite side of the car and pretended there was nothing around as she couldn't see the bird. A few steps beyond the car she froze into a beautiful point, held while I flushed the bird, and her five minute lesson was complete. Ten minutes later I was parked on Mrs. Alton-Smyth's immaculate driveway listening to her exclaim how rushed she was to get to a luncheon and admiring her two aged thoroughbred mares at the same time.

"I'll have to put on a twitch and a sideline in order to do a rectal exam," I explained.

Aghast, she said, "Oh I've been working around them for days and I'm sure they won't kick!"

I asked quietly, "How often during the day do you stand where I will have to stand and examine them rectally?"

At this she blushed, and held the twitch.

A twitch is a loop of chain on the end of a stick that is put around the upper lip and turned snugly to control the horse. I instruct people to use no pain unless the horse seems to be mischievous and then only to apply pressure briefly. They should allow the horse to understand that the control will stop if he stands quietly. People who fear either the animal or the situation twist tightly and hold. Nothing in the world panics any species of animal as much as confinement. Boss Lady found this out by hugging a frightened animal thereby supplying the final stress that caused it to fight, bite, and claw to freedom.

The plastic sleeves I use for rectal examinations are a boon to mankind if used correctly. From an ecological point of view they are abominable and I'm careful how I dispose of them. I have seen them used on cows, dropped in the manure drop, sent to the field and spread with the manure, baled up with the hay and then, when the bale is fed the next winter, they end up in front of the cattle only to be casually picked up and thrown in the manure gutter to start their yearly cycle again. Considering their inorganic indestructibility this could go on for years.

At this moment I lubricated the sleeve and commenced the rectal exam. I found the ovary and from there passed my hand beneath the uterus from left to right looking for a telltale bulge. Both mares were non-pregnant or "open" in stockmen's terms.

Mrs. Alton-Smyth was disappointed. She said, "What's the matter with them?"

The genital tracts were normal and the people who called them pregnant were probably only guessing.

"The mares will probably be showing heat soon, as they all start this time of year in this hemisphere. When they do, call and we will see about breeding them," I said.

I also suggested that she didn't have to look a gift horse in the mouth next time but she damn well better take a good look at the uterus.

I repacked my equipment and wheeled out of her drive past an impressive house and barn and sped down the road. Mr. Stonecold's farm was ten miles away and time was short as it was now eleven o'clock. I forced myself to stop to make out the charge slip and felt the warm sun pouring through the windshield. Ahead of me in a wall corner stood an old ash tree and I remembered a summer noon in a similar place at my grandfather's farm many years ago. I had met a visiting girl who had long strong legs, high cheek bones, black hair and green eyes. This type of girl I always looked for ever since I had been in love with my music teacher in public school at the age of eight. In the sun this spring day I had kissed the visitor, an act which exhausted all my courage, and told her I had joined the Marine Corps to fight the Japanese and would be leaving in a week and would she mind if I wrote to her as I didn't have anyone else to write to. She said okay so I decided I would marry her at some future date though I didn't tell her that.

Mr. Stonecold is one of the old school, much to the detriment of his animals. They are just barely fed, beaten regularly because the owner is bitter and has "little man fever". This syndrome is seen among men of small stature and is an aggressive, cynical state of mind that manifests itself very strongly when someone six foot three like me is around even if I say nothing. I had walked in on this old horned toad in the middle of his having a bowel movement, poised, native-like, over the manure gutter. This, of course, is against state law as well as being primitive, predisposing to human parasitism, and downright shocking. His daddy did it before him and he wasn't going to change. I was glad none of the girls that often ride with me was there today.

"Well, here's the big tall clean doctor in white, late as usual!" he said with a cynical smile that could turn bright if I took offense...

"I'm sorry but I didn't get up until late and two lady horse owners wanted me to share coffee in bed with them this morning," I told him.

"Heh!" he snorted. "Don't doubt it a damned bit."

I proceeded to inject tuberculin into twenty-five head of these, manure caked cattle. I made an injection between skin layers in the tail fold and also one in the lip of the vulva while my friend walked along trying to get me into conversations covering local issues and gossip and not helping me hold the cattle still. I then took down ear tag numbers and replaced one or two lost tags and designated the age and breed of the cattle. I would return in seventy-two hours to check the injection sites for swelling, and if I found any I'd brand and condemn the animal for slaughter.

I was packing to leave when my warm friend said, "Say, while you're here take a look at a cup'la feet for me, wud-ja?"

I knew it was late but I went in and looked at feet on two cows that had obviously had trouble for a month. Mr. Stonecold's opinion of "vetrinaries" was one of suspicion and resentment and he really only knew two diagnoses; milk fever and calving trouble. All other variations from normal were expected acts of God and could be ignored.

"These are long standing problems," I said. "I'll leave some time to help them when I return."

48

"I suppose you're havin' lunch with that good looking rich lady," he growled, not believing me.

Knowing full well there would be no lunch that day, I said brightly, "Say, that's a great idea. I forgot about her. I'll call Marie and tell her I can't make it and head the other way!"

I left him standing in the driveway in front of the broken down barn, convinced I was a sex maniac, and headed down the valley at twelve-ten for my date at Mrs. Meany's. I was sure at that moment that TB testing must be the end of the professional trail and once more swore adamantly that I would give it up "next year" and see if I couldn't get the state to hire medical assistants to do it.

I slowed my car beside a spring freshet that bounced down the grey hillside. Shafts of sun revealed the small blossoms of bloodroot as they pushed their way through the decaying leaves. Along the black water of the brook new green noses of skunk cabbage jeered from between mossy sticks. I stopped for three minutes in order to wash from my boots and my hands the filth of Mr. Stonecold's farm and to let the sun and sounds of Spring wash from my mind the lingering useless tone of a bitter man's voice.

Refreshed and draped in fresh white coveralls, I sped down the valley and reported in on the radio.

"Some doctor called and said he couldn't make it this noon and would you be his agent er sumthin'?" my lady-love nurse rasped over the airways.

"Okay. Then I *will* be on time for office hours," I answered.

49

She keyed the mike only to groan, "Jeez - I'll never get done."

I continued on to meet with three officials of the neighboring town gathered at Mrs. Meany's "kennel".

Our subsequent tour through a choking atmosphere of seven unlit rooms filled with dog waste, spoiled food, and fifty-seven creatures all begging for recognition produced three men as close to being horror stricken as possible. I immediately had help to bring about the condemnation of the building. A phone call and a following letter started the machinery I needed to rid the community of these cancerous living quarters.

A brief conference of all the men in front of the house brought the opinion that all would try but probably things would go unchanged in the end. I was invited for coffee, and although I knew this to be the common call to conference for all salaried and politically appointed people, it was after one and I had to drive to office hours. I was hungry and thought perhaps I could grab something to eat before I was pounced upon by Boss Lady or an anxious client, or by Guenivere, my soft spoken super secretary. A month later I was relieved to learn Mrs. Meany's puppy well was closed by town officials.

While cruising up the familiar valley I noticed the sunlight produced a soft almost humming suede on the hardwood hillsides caused by the millions of ripening buds soon to burst into Spring and the people had begun to move in their customary mid-day pattern. The resident state-trooper who watched me carefully was headed home for lunch with his new bride waved

50

happily as did the town clerk on her usual walk of a block to her home and lunch. The first selectman talked in front of the barber shop with its owner and the really friendly and enjoyable proprietor of the package store. The conversation was, I'm sure, of the horse races in the city and not of politics. On the flats near the river, work was progressing on the expensive new school that echoed the growing population in this once remote valley. Plans for a new school of the same capacity costing about half and at bond interest of about one percent less were voted down five years before when I was school board chairmen. It was unhappily defeated, not so much by the expected frantic minority with valley-bound minds that voted no, but more so by those with more worldly informed minds who thought it was the obvious course to take and stayed home with no "yes" votes because they thought it was a sure thing.

The people all waved or nodded, or with fake dramatics ran and hid behind poles in mock fear and graphic comment on the way I pilot my great machine. There are those who frown as I pass, waiting for the day when they can say, "I knew it would happen". The wait has now been twenty-five years and more miles than they will travel in their lives. I am happy, strong, and confident as a functioning part of an animal community and maybe would be singled out to be of interest when viewed by some gigantic being through a giant microscope. It is possible, you know!

****

51

CHAPTER THREE: Monday afternoon

The hunger that kneaded my stomach subsided with a resolute sigh as I turned in my drive and saw two cars already waiting at my clinic. One, I realized, was unknown, but happily, the other belonged to that friend of all men, Mr. Bruce Watson.

Mr., or Dr. Watson as I called him, was a man of exquisite taste in clothing, food, and wine. He was raised in the era of great writers like Fitzgerald, Maugham, and Hemingway, was a railroad buff and the possessor of an independent income that kept him comfortable. His round, mature, ruddy face always glowed with scrubbed perfection and an almost constant smile glowed beneath prominent eyes that always in a flash reminded me of the five Pekinese he kept. From beneath well formed shoulders and adequate chest there flowed an ample and expected belly, the result of really good food for a life time, and this mass was held up by stocky legs that moved in an agile way which belied his years. His clothes were always of ageless quiet good taste. Checked woolen slacks, slightly baggy, tattersall or red flannel vest, checked shirts, and a bow tie, practically always gloves, and shoes of such excellent leather that years of polishing gave depth to their luster. His hat today was a Sherlock Holmes "deer stalker" that only in midwinter was replaced by a Russian type mouton. He often stopped in at this time of day with something to discuss about his dogs, local developments, or world events, and he usually stayed through the emotional montage of vignettes that took place at office hours. He was an animal man and his understanding small talk with clients or their animals often lightened a difficult situation. His old world, polite manner of answering my busy telephone kept anxious or irate clients happily at bay while I finished some tense chore. His appetite for living was fed, as was mine, by the acceptance of people's problems and by following through and digesting each medical case and its attendant varying emotional concern of the owner.

"Hello, Doctor," he said striding from the clinic door as I gathered my blood and manure laden used coveralls from the trunk. "You've been off in the hills loafing again, I see!"

"Glad to see you, Watson, my boy," I said and laughed. "I suppose you've been clipping coupons all morning or have you been tea-ing with some sexy dowager?"

"That you will never know," he remarked as he held the door open for me.

The phone rang as I came into the waiting room and a pleasant looking old lady stood up and said, "Tigger and I came early so we could be first." Mrs. Hyphen's eyes lowered to my stained coveralls, not with a quick recovery, smiled with just a wrinkled nose to show where her mind had been and said, "Here's my little Tigger again."

Tigger sat with a slit-eyed wariness on the bench and all but dared me to touch him. It didn't even occur to Mrs. Hyphen that I hadn't eaten as she had never missed a meal in her life, but "Tigger knew I was hungry and was happy about it.

53

"I'll be right there, Ma'm," I said as I entered my office and heaved my coveralls towards the laundry room. Gwen, my secretary waited quietly with the phone, and as I took it she went to get my white coat.

The voice on the phone said, "How much to "spade" a dog, Doc? The bastard's in heat again."

"Thirty-five dollars, but don't do it while she's in heat."

"Jesus, it's cheaper to shoot her!" the deep feeling voice said.

"That's up to you, Sir," I said and hung the phone up, not too quietly.

Gwen handed me a lab report on the white terrier as I headed for the examining room and the scintillating Mrs. Hyphen. I read it as I was walking and the thirty-five thousand white count with twenty band cells pinned down the diagnosis of pyometra; surgery NOW.

I lifted a growling Tigger to the table and noticed he was dripping urine. The telephone was ringing and three more people entered the waiting room. Dr. Watson had been talking to Mrs. Hyphen and held the dog while I was pulling on a plastic glove. A quick rectal exam, surprising to Tigger, shocking to Mrs. Hyphen, and humorous to Dr. Watson (who smiled at the client) revealed a still enlarged prostate. As I was preparing an injection to halt the inflammation, Mrs. Hyphen described the symptoms. Meantime I gave the poodle the injection noting that Dr. Watson's knuckles were white while he, still smiling at Mrs. Hyphen, tried to keep little Tigger from ripping off my arm. Mrs. Hyphen talked on as I reached for the telephone that had been set on the window connecting to Gwen's office.

Covering the telephone I said, "Take Tigger home and give him some of these pills with brandy each night, please."

I answered the phone and reached for the urinary sedative pills on the shelf. The voice said, "We got another new foal, Doc. I been tryin' to reach you all morning."

I had spent many hours convincing the man on the other end of the phone that I should see each new-born foal, and I knew the call meant another thirty-mile round trip before bed that night.

"Right. See you before nightfall."

"I leave at five, Doc."

Mrs. Hyphen was just finishing a long sentence with, "I do hope he'll be all right. Unknown to the lady, Tigger was at the other end of the leash disdainfully urinating on my instrument stand as she spoke. I noted a full flow of urine and answered, "He's going to live a long time. Let me see him in two weeks."

She went out happily, having completed her trip for the day, and a young couple carrying a new puppy came in followed by an obese painted woman carrying a red Pekinese.

By holding the waiting room door I motioned to the young couple to come in while smiling at Mrs. Hyphen who spoke a torrent of clichés and was not hearing a word. The girl carried a small brown puppy whose fearful expression matched her own and the young man glanced at me semi-defiantly, committed to guiding his "family" through the insecurity of an unfamiliar world. It is almost a predictable period of time after the first flush of physical pleasures has subsided in a new marriage that so many new couples acquire a puppy or kitten. The desire for a baby image or complete family is so powerful that the husband usually purchases something for his quietly pressuring wife.

"Oh, my goodness - just like a real hospital," the wide-eyed girl said. "Look, Dear, they have x-rays and everything."

I sometimes think that people have some rather weird images of veterinarians after I hear things like that and after paying for all my equipment that services animals. It's not that different from human equipment. I feel little quirks of wonder inside me how people can't understand that animals have hearts, lungs, kidneys, bones, genital organs, intestines, hormones, brains, teeth, and eyes. all of which can malfunction in the same way humans do. I'm sure before the girl came in she was afraid she was casting her puppy-baby at the mercy of some old crumb that practiced with a jackknife and a bottle of turpentine. Sensitive to her fear, I cuddled her puppy and talked to it knowing that this would put her at ease most rapidly. Her husband noticeably relaxed as he realized I was human. The phone that I hadn't heard ring was placed on the office window signifying a call was waiting. Boss Lady was not-so-silently hurling invectives at Tigger as she mopped in the corner and the young couple began to tighten again as they listened in wonderment.

"Get me a vaccine, please," I said as I reached for the phone.

"Soon's I finish what I'm doin' here," said Boss Lady. "Why do boy dogs always have to do that?"

Unknown to herself she was the original women's liberationist and disliked all male tendencies in dogs, especially those with sexual overtones.

Mr. Watson's top Peke, Charlie, possessed an unquavering libido and carried off the sexual act with the same frequency and aplomb that men use in simply tipping their hats. Boss Lady tolerated Charlie but shook her head in anger at his sexual athletics.

The voice on the phone asked, "How much to alter my dog and keep him from roaming?"

By the question I knew it was a male and he wasn't worried about roaming. They were shopping around to veterinarians for the best price. To get things going I asked, "Is he riding the children?"

The stunned silence at the other end gulped, "Yeah, Doc. Isn't it best to alter a dog like that?"

"No," I answered." He'll outgrow it and you'd be sorry if you did it because you wouldn't end up with a dog. Just a fat blob."

"Thanks a lot!" he said relieved. "I'll tell the little woman." The "little woman" I'm sure was a little smarter than he, went to church every Sunday, probably was president of the PTA and was opposed to sex-education.

The girl by the table cuddled the dog as I spoke, and when I hung up she handed me a printed paper with a shaky hand. The look in her eyes was exactly the same as the frightened puppy's. I knew that the compassion that welled within me must remain unspoken because this girl needed confidence in strength and know-how, not the same song that her husband would give to her and she would give to the puppy. The paper I knew was a contract of sale that came from a pet shop guaranteeing the puppy if it was examined by a veterinarian within forty-eight hours after purchase. The guarantee would replace the puppy if I found it defective. This, of course, was better than the virus laden dogs that came from pet shops in years past, but still not enough. In the whirlwind of potential dollars surrounding the sale such things as incubation periods, diseases go unrecognized and puppies often sicken and die at about two weeks after emotionally hungry children, young women, and older couples whose children are gone acquire them and circle their worlds around them. This is especially depressing at Christmas time when the turnover in puppies is fast but does allow a few days to harvest some viruses at a gathering place in some pet shop window.

Boss Lady slammed the icebox door and came in with the vaccine. The look on her face put Frankenstein to shame until she saw the puppy and melted with an, "Awwww that's pure love. Look at that, Doc." She swept the delicate creature up in her arms with honest emotion and the puppy immediately wet the front of her lab coat. From the look of consternation on the girl's face I kind of thought she was wetting her pants at the same time. She soon was caught up by Boss Lady's honesty and breathed a sigh of relief to find a partner in group compassion. I vaccinated the puppy with a prayer that his immune response would win the race with whatever viruses were lurking there and looked him over for congenital defects and parasites.

"Please bring in a stool sample soon," I said as I was again going towards a waiting phone.

"Huh?" said the husband.

Boss Lady helped in admirable fashion: "When he messes on the rug put it in a jar and bring it here."

With a look like he had just gotten a glass of hot beer at the American Legion weekly get-together he blurted, "Oh, okay. Let's go, Honey."

The warm happy couple left passing the painted woman in the waiting room. She hugged her big red Peke and frowned at the boy and girl. She *just knew* that puppy had some disease to give her dog and she *just knew* the kids were going home to make love.

I finally remembered that her name was Hemogram..Miss Isabel Hemogram. She was a laboratory technician at the nearby mental institution. Miss H. came in about every six weeks, each time having learned a new set of symptoms of a syndrome new to her or the intricacies of a new laboratory test that she secretly hoped to catch me on. Prepared to engage in a battle of wits I said with my best "comrades-in-destiny" air, "Good afternoon, Nurse."

With a flicker of real pride in her cold eyes beneath a serious frown she hoarsely whispered, "Hello, Doctor. I think we have a real problem here," and shuffled her great bulk through the door.

"What's the matter?" I asked.

"Looks like a C-A of the bowel to me, Doctor," she said in her best hospital lingo. "I think we ought to run a sed rate and a serum transaminase, don't you?"

"Well, maybe," I answered. "What's he doing that you don't like the looks of?"

"He's been anemic, I'm sure, and I've been feeding liver and giving B-12 shots for two weeks. Now he seems logy and uncomfortable and his BMs are very black. I figure it's blood and I'm sure we are dealing with a carcinoma."

The large red Peke, who was obviously used to being poked and prodded in both professional and amateur medical investigations, sat and stared straight ahead as if under the influence of his native poppy-juice. A normal dog in this situation would be apprehensive but this one, named Tut-Tut, remained relaxed while I felt all his abdominal organs and listened with a cold stethoscope to various sighs and gurglings. Miss Hemogram eyed Bruce Watson with the stern air of a communist interrogator as he observed the dog with a practiced eye.

"A good looking Peke," he ventured.

"He's a champion and his ancestry goes back to the original palace guard dogs. I raised him from three weeks old. I'm using him for stud again next week. Be careful. He's nervous. He doesn't like men. He doesn't feel well. I think he has something organic."

Mr. Watson's normally prominent eyes invaded a little more space in the room as he received this barrage that left no doubt about the woman's superior knowledge of Pekedom. He turned to me surreptitiously mouthing the words, "Organic, Doctor!"

Gwen placed the phone on the window ledge again. Since I figured the best way to get to it was to give Miss H. something to do, I inserted a thermometer in the dog and asked her to watch it. Again, with professional pride, she looked at her masculine nurse's watch and as her arm encircled the dog he immediately made sexual advances towards it.

"I know, Baby, I love you to," said Miss Isabel.

Mr. Watson's eyes flickered to mine aghast but bemused. Boss Lady frowned in the corner. I reached for the phone, noticing the young couple outside stuck in a traffic jam of three or four cars that had arrived in my parking lot. Before answering I asked Boss Lady to get two packaged enemas from the drug room mainly to break up the embarrassing scene and asked Miss Hemogram to think of all the medication used in the past week. I motioned a thumb towards the parking lot to Mr. Watson and trying to sound unhurried I said "Hello" to the phone.

"Hi, Doc," a rough male voice said. "We have a tough situation here. I just had to shoot a dog that ripped up a guy pretty bad. If I brought the body up would you decapitate it and cremate the remains? I have to take the head to the lab tomorrow to check for rabies."

"Yes, I can. What happened?"

"This guy's mother-in-law asked him to feed the dog while she was in the hospital. He went in the house and the dog went for

61

him. The animal was frantic and we had to shoot it or it would have starved 'cause nobody could get near it."

"Oh," I said, feeling inside a powerful pang of pity for an animal whose world had gone awry with his beloved mistress gone and who died doing the job his simple mind told him to do-- protect his territory. "I'll see you later."

"Right." He hung up and I turned again to Tut-Tut.

"I gave him two buffered aspirin a day for a week and a tranquilizer every evening," Miss Hemogram blurted as I turned away from the phone.

"Isobel," I said while no one was in the room, "you have effectively poisoned and constipated your dog. The black stool is from the liver, the tranquilizers have slowed the bowel, and with no bulk he is severely constipated. The aspirin has reached a dangerous level and please do as I ask or Tut-Tut is going to be one sick pup!"

Miss Hemogram narrowed her eyes and said, "Doctor, I'm sure if you run a sed rate and a transaminase you will find trouble!"

I'll do that if he's sicker in three days. Right now he is going to get an enema and some decent food."

Boss Lady careened through the door and I sent her and Miss Hemogram eagerly into the ward room to perform the delicate medical task, both frowning, both happy to be technically involved, both highly wary of each other.

Mr. Watson came back from straightening out the traffic jam and with him was a very fine gentleman, Mr. Forest Field, in poplin pants, elegant flannel shirt, well-worn high quality hunting shoes, and leading an aged but aristocratic pointer. The man I knew well and the dog I had known for years as a fine grouse dog. Mr. Field's ice blue eyes swept politely from his conversation and held mine for a quivering instant, then returned to Mr. Watson. A month before I had x-rayed the pointer's leg and lungs, and verified the diagnosis of bone cancer which had spread to lung tissue. I advised him to take the superbly trained animal home and spoil him until he was no longer comfortable, then bring him to me for a quiet death.

Those who have not trained and hunted over a good bird dog can never know the extent of communication and affectionate respect that exists between a man and his hunting companion, but the emotion is as deep as any that exists. An eye-to-eye exchange of information and excitement flickers between the two as they warily approach good game cover. Extreme discomfort is born with ease as they share bits of food in hasty shelter from cold autumn rain on the hillsides. On long car rides to and from the hunt the man speaks his thoughts and the wise animal appears to listen and occasionally glance towards the speaker though he knows only that the voice tone indicates that all is well. When a sensitive man faces the crises of life that occur inevitably in later years, a dog of this caliber senses minute changes in movement and atmosphere about his master and presses his body against the man's legs. The action, because of the basic animal liason that has existed in the hunt field, far surpasses the well meant platitudes of old friends or the proffered, necessarily hackneyed actions and words of a local minister.

So it was with Mr. Field who had in the past year lost a beloved wife and had seen his daughter's marriage torn apart because of the homosexual preferences of his son-in-law. He now must face the death of his cherished dog with grace and honor, and somehow, in the chaos of the day I must help him without appearing to.

"Hi, Mr. Field. Hello, Thor." I said. "Come on in."

A slight frowning glance at Mr. Watson was all that was needed to signal a tense situation, thanks to Bruce's sensitivity. Bruce launched immediately into a running conversation as I stooped to scratch Thor's ears. In lifting the wasting dog to the table I could feel his difficult breathing and see the anxious look in his eye.

"Careful of that dog's rectum," reverberated from the other room as an imperious Miss Hemogram gave orders to an imperious Boss Lady.

"You just watch your end of this guy and I'll watch mine," came the raucous answer. "I've done this more times than you've changed your stockings!"

"Not on people," squawked the *Lady in White*.

"This ain't people," Boss Lady proclaimed, and my confidence in her ability kept me silent.

"Mr. Field," I said, "people differ a great deal at a time like this. Some want to stay, some want to leave. Some want the body to bury, and some can't be bothered or want only to be in

64

contact while there is life. Some want to take ashes. What do you want, Sir?"

This powerful man looked me in the eye and said, "I will stay until he is gone and then I will leave him to you."

I recognized an awareness of life in the man that dictated no ceremony. People that want ceremonious pet burials of ashes of cadavers are not cognizant of biological end points and worry mostly about the impact of death upon their own image and usually savor and need the attendant emotional bath.

Mr. Watson compressed the vein for me as Thor looked for reassurance and found it in Mr. Field's quiet touch and the instant I sent home the lethal barbiturate, the two women appeared from the other room.

"Are you putting that beautiful dog to sleep?" Boss Lady blurted.

Without looking up I said, "Get out of here," and in shocked silence the two nurses stalked out of the room.

Slowly the glowing light of his world comprehension died in Thor's eyes and he quietly laid his head upon Mr. Field's weather-wrinkled hand, content with its familiar feel.

"Please hunt with me this Fall, Mr. Field," I said. "I have a good dog and she and I both have a lot to learn."

He nodded in the affirmative and, choking out a hoarsely whispered, "Thanks, Doc," turned and left. I fought back tears and being unsuccessful, turned to the sink to borrow time in washing the syringe. I could not enjoy the luxury of giving in to, and therefore unburdening myself of these emotions as I had to

65

continue working. My apparent coldness in these situations sometimes gains for me a reputation of insensitivity.

The telephone rang and a petulant Boss Lady returned bearing a hurt expression for having been chased out of the room. A noisy, barking shepherd entered the waiting-room leading a house wife with three young kids, and a lady with a cat carrier followed at a safe distance. I motioned the lady with the cat directly into the office and turned to face the protestations of the lady with the shepherd.

"Hey, I was first!" she said, "and I got real problems. This dog's itchin' bad so's we can't hardly watch television. My Joe says to get it fixed or put her outa the way."

I was, of course, deeply touched by the gravity of her television problems, but asked please to let me get the cat out of the office first.

"Oh, okay," she agreed. "I gotta get the kids to the Doctor's at four though, so hurry."

Her burden to her was as severe as Mr. Field's was to him and I had to treat it that way even though Thor's body in the ward room rattled me to my very soul. I smiled, closed the door and turned to face the elderly lady with the cat carrier and was reminded of the phone waiting by Boss Lady. She was standing with it in her hand like the Statue of Liberty.

"Hello there, Mrs. Bee!" I exclaimed as I reached for the phone. She unfolded a written list of questions and started talking not noting at all that a caller was waiting.

"Matilda hasn't been right since you spayed her two years ago and I thought I would bring her in for a check up," she insinuated.

"How's my bitch?" asked a strong female voice from the phone part way to my ear.

I strove to remember her voice that I obviously was supposed to recognize and wondered which of the four bitches that were in at the time was hers.

"Did she have pyometra?"

Then I remembered the white terrier and said, "She is scheduled for surgery in half an hour."

"You haven't operated yet? Why'd I bring her in on Saturday?"

"So that I could pin down the diagnosis and prepare her for surgery," I countered.

"Oh. Can I call about five to get a report?"

Knowing I would be on the road then but not wanting to go through the explanations of things I had to do, and conscious also of people's tendency to believe that theirs was the only case that day, I said yes, hoping that our next phone contact would be about ten o'clock that night.

"Thank you. Now you save her, Understand? She's a champion!"

I put down the phone to face Mrs. Bee's second question (she didn't even know I had answered the phone) and wondered what it is in people that makes them think a champion dog should get different treatment from a dog-dog.

67

"---------------and she goes to her kitty box all the time and just sits and sits," said Mrs. Bee. "I read a book by a cat-handler and it says that this is bladder inflammation and needs to be treated with," (she consults her notes), "anti-bi-oh-tics and something to change the PH, whatever that is, of her urine. Do you have those things?"

As she spoke my hand was probing the lovely cat's abdomen and she purred, exhibiting worry, intelligence, and confidence in people all in one purr.

"Your cat is constipated," I said.

"But the book says----"

"I know," I interrupted, "but the symptoms are the same from your point of view as she is straining in her cat box in the same way as she would for cystitis. What are you feeding her?"

"I offer her lots of things but she only eats fish and dried cat food," she answered.

"You must get her on other food," I said, knowing the problem. Cats can melt a person that doesn't really know them just by refusing to eat until they get what they like. Most people, because they are human, cannot combat the cold disdain practiced unfeelingly by their pets. They usually give in to feeding weird diets contributing freely to an eventual problem a veterinarian is asked to handle. Compassion again takes its toll! The majority of "disease" that we as veterinarians are asked to deal with are actually caused by domestication.

"How?" asked Mrs. Bee...

68

One is left at this point with a choice of words. Either you say *"starve her,"* or you say *"withhold food,"* depending on the personality with which you a faced. I made my choice.

"Withhold any food until she will eat a good dog food," I said. "Canned dog foods are the result of a good deal more research than are cat foods. They are really good for your cat."

There was at this point a war whoop from the waiting room as Boss Lady encountered the shepherd. I looked up in time to see her advancing on the dog with nothing on her mind but hugging it. The animal could only see a menacing creature advancing and, since it was on a chain and limited in movement, it bared its fangs and snarled.

"I just wanted to love 'um," said a shocked Boss Lady, really unable to understand the animal's objective attitude.

She came through the door from the waiting room accompanied by Mr. Watson and the yelling of the kids waiting to come in and investigate yet another room.

Mrs. Bee's wise cat sat unperturbed on the table quietly awaiting a decision from "people" and Mrs. Bee fluttered out having been told that the constipation was severe and should be handled in the hospital. Mr. Watson ushered her out the door, Boss Lady whisked the quiet cat to the ward, the shepherd and its entourage blustered in, and once again Gwen placed the phone down on the sill.

I had just said hello and a breathless distant voice urgently started to tell me that she had gotten fly-repellent in her horse's eyes and they were blue when Boss Lady roared back into the room asking loudly for the name of the cat's owner for the hospital record, and the kids tripped over my tipsy instrument stand with a crash. I hastily told the horse's owner to give me her drugstore's number in the distant town and assured her that all would be okay if she followed my instructions given to the pharmacist.

"Blue on an eye is analogous to red on skin," I told the girl and calmed her fear about her horse going blind.

"But my boyfriend's horse has a blue eye and he's blind," she wailed.

I knew the horse and said, "That is a cataract. It's a lot different. Give me the number, please, and get to the drug store."

I repeated the number as given and Gwen wrote it down. After the girl hung up I asked Gwen to call the drugstore and turned to face the snarling shepherd and kids waiting to see me bitten.

The dog was typical of many of the German breeds. Insecure and frightened into aggression, the end product of a complete lack of animal sense on the owner's part and raising dogs for dollars alone on the breeder's part. I'm sure they had dreams of a Rin Tin Tin when they bought their shepherd but, like so many, they ended up with a maladjusted, mentally misaligned misfit whose scared yellow eyes dared me to make one move.

"Give me the leash," I said.

"He'll bite if you get close," the lady said.

"Not if I have the leash," I said as I took it and ordered the dog to walk with me. I tugged the lead firmly, patted the dog strongly on the ribcage, and was pleased to see a softening in his baleful eyes as he recognized someone to trust. Up to this point in his life he had been handled by giggling kids, a woman so scared of him that she fed him as a sort of offering to the devil, and a man who understood only motors and pro football.

While lifting the dog to the table he urinated and defecated in sheer panic. As I spoke to calm him he wagged his tail splashing urine from the table into the smiling, entranced faces of the children. I was pleased and pretended not to notice and motioned Boss Lady to move in and handle the dog while I prepared an injection to treat his dermatitis.

"What do you feed the animal?" I asked.

"I give him whatever is on sale at the supermarket," said the lady as she adjusted her curlers. "Most of 'em I see on TV ads."

I am almost sure that if television offered it at fairly regular intervals, about eight-five percent of the human race would go back to human sacrifice as a protection from bad weather.

I gave the dog an injection as the children gasped. My friend, the dog, did not know anything was going to happen and hence really didn't feel it but the children's reactions brought fear again into his eyes. I suggested they add meat to his diet, plus some vitamins and minerals and let them know the office call was over by reaching for the phone which had found its way back to the sill.

The shepherd dog started out the door, returning once more to a familiar chattering world, but hesitated for a moment to

71

glance at me with a question, affection, and slight yearning in his eyes. For a fleeting time he had known strength and understanding. He desperately wanted more. The knot was turned a little tighter inside me.

The pharmacist in the distant town was on the phone and took my prescription for the horse's eye medicine. Since his reaction was one of humor about treating a horse I told him to be sure and get the directions correct and snapped out my government registration number just to remind him that mine is a profession and the horse meant as much to its owner as any person would.

I turned from the phone and found Gwen waiting for me to do office work, which I hated, Mr. Watson anticipating a conversation finally, and Boss Lady busily setting up the x-ray. She had noisily retrieved the stand from a closet where she preferred to keep it in arrogant but silent disagreement with her counterpart who worked the other half of the week. That lady preferred to keep it handily astride the sterilizer.

"We won't be x-raying today," I said. "Set up for surgery and warm up Ringers solution and five percent dextrose for intravenous therapy."

"You've got to x-ray that poor puppy that was hit this morning," said Boss Lady, who was hungrily waiting for this emotional outburst since she first realized, a half hour before, that time was fleeting and I would pull some kind of deal. She had purposely not told me of the pup so that she could savor the sweet succulence of one-upsmanship on me. I had seen the pup and felt

72

his cracked pelvis in a fast trip through the ward as I had placed Thor's body in the tub.

"Oh yes," I said. "He has a cracked pelvis. Put a mat in his cage and get me a half cc of that pain-killing drug I use."

"Good Gawd!" she said as she clumsily hauled the stand back to the closet. "That poor baby--and that doctor really doesn't give a damn!"

I gave the white terrier an injection of a pre-anesthetic sedative and retired to my office for a brief session of signing checks, checking invoices, reading rapidly about new drugs, throwing out trash mail from travel bargains to sexual literature, and finding again that my balance was about fourteen hundred dollars. My bills amounted to twenty-three hundred and my accounts receivable were about thirty-two hundred dollars. The country was, as usual, running tenuously on credit fostered by banks backing credit cards. People venture forth armed with credit cards, as they were told by radio and television, to vacations at motels and resorts. When the momentarily forgotten bills come in at the end of the month there is, of course, no recourse other than to strike for higher wages as they simply can't meet the cost of "living".

Hidden in the pile of mail were two communications. One a card with a pencil drawing of a horse's head. Underneath, a teenager's printing said, "Thank you for saving my 'Timmy' the other night." On the back is printed in red pencil "Hall Mark". The other brief letter, in delicate feminine handwriting, is an invitation to dinner, "etc." to discuss horse breeding because she

73

is new in the field and wants to do things right. My body and mind as one vibrant force remembered this woman. A rumble of passion started in my groin sending an instant's flash of memory to my head.

The temperature at the horse show had been well over a hundred degrees that day and as usual I had been bored and irritated by the fact that I was required by rules to remain at the show. A very beautiful horse bumped into me outside the show ring and a brunette girl riding it had apologized. I had seen her at many shows, admired her in a male animal way, and knew her name was Tara Something. Finally the show ended and I had gone to my woodland cabin to shower, and when night arrived I lit a fire in the deep fireplace for company. Then I fell asleep.

The pine forest is thick here and I know it well---well enough to awaken when night noises changed in response to an intruder. In the glowing firelight this tall girl stood dressed only in tight canary riding breeches and black boots. The shadows accentuated her breasts and hair and the flickering light gave them each a sensuous movement.

"Hello, Tara," I said softly. "How did you find me?"

"Your friends respond to a smile," she said with a glint in her eye. "Come help me with my boots."

"I have nothing on," I said a little nervously.

"Come---I was counting on that!" was her reply.

I stood as she pulled down her breeches and sank softly to the floor raising one booted leg. I grasped the boot and pulled it off, then the second boot and she followed with breeches and likewise pants in one smooth motion. She sat for a moment before me with the firelight playing on the inside of her thighs and, bracing both hands on the floor behind her, looked up at me.

"Doctor, I've watched you for a long time. I hope you don't mind this intrusion but I like the look of you," she whispered softly. Her hands were sliding up the back of my legs finally resting on my buttocks where they gripped firmly and the warmth of her lips and hair closed in on my body. The night closed in on us both.

*****

"Do you want to pay the February bills this week or not?"

It was Gwen bringing me from a second's memory back to the office and I looked quickly at the totals and said to pay all February bills that she could, starting with the small businessmen and going up to the big companies, a method I have followed for fifteen years.

"That was a shame about that pointer, Doctor," said Mr. Watson. "What was the matter?"

"Osteogenic sarcoma," I answered covering my emotions by using a big name.

The phone rang and I grabbed it. "Do you think you could do a vasectomy on my guinea pig?" a female voice asked.

"Wouldn't castration be all right?" I asked. I wasn't sure I could tell the sperm duct from a nerve at that size.

"Well, I want him to make love but I can't have any more baby guinea pigs!"

Buying time I asked her to call in twenty-four hours. I don't like to refuse people but I hoped to find some research time. As I hung up I remembered I had to order some vaccines, so I held down the receiver with one hand as I tried to recall the drug company's number. Sedation time was passing on the terrier, Mr. Watson was on the verge of bursting out with some new thought, Gwen stood with two letters to sign, and Boss Lady screamed from the other room, "Well everything is ready for your special blue-blood dog. What Ya' sittin' around doin' nothing for?"

She obviously didn't know how serious the terrier's problem was.

Ten minutes later found me standing over the terrier with intravenous tubing attached to a needle in her jugular. I, as a veterinary surgeon, must watch depth of anesthesia and degree of shock while monitoring intravenous therapy and doing meticulous surgery - and still come out as successful as the teams of surgeons and nurses do on television and in fables. Under these circumstances of not much help I am astounded at the numbers we, as veterinarians, save and appalled that often the only ones we hear of again are those that we lose.

"What's that?" asked a shocked Mr. Watson as my latex sheathed hands opened the abdomen.

"Uterus, believe it or not," I answered. "With this problem its mass may make up one tenth of the body weight and it is filled with puss and debris, making the animal a great deal more toxic than it appears!"

I lifted the organ and with clamp and ligatures on vessels, removed it en masse and sewed the abdomen after filling it with warm saline.

The phone rang and Gwen said it was the owner of the quarter horse yearling making sure I hadn't forgotten. The office bell rang and a uniformed man entered reminding me of the dog the warden had shot. I removed my gloves and dropped the bloody drape, then wrapped the dog firmly. After giving it two injections I hoped would ward off shock, I told Gwen to tell the warden to bring in the dog's body while I changed into coveralls and adjusted my mind to farm calls again. I had done my best with the terrier and now my mind must go to other things. I was leaving the post-operative terrier in Boss Lady's competent hands though a similar case in human medicine would be watched by doctors and nurses for twenty-four hours. Such are the economics of veterinary medicine. I know very well what should be done but must move to the next case as swiftly as possible in order to care for all I am asked to and to pay the mortgage.

In the ward room when I returned there stood the two wardens, and in the tub lay a black dog with blood oozing from a chest wound. I took my shiny knife, quickly severed the head, and placed it in a plastic bag.

"What happened to that old bastard?" queried one warden looking at Thor's body. I resented his tone because of Thor's unforgettable personality but realized the warden couldn't know that.

"He was an old friend and dying of cancer so I put him to sleep." I knew the man would get the message.

In passing back through the surgery I noticed the phone on the sill and picked it up, "Yes, sorry to make you wait."

"Well, are ya' comin' or ain't ya'? I got these two colts penned up finally!" The voice obviously figured I had been torn from a chair in front of the TV set.

"Just leaving, Ben. Be a half hour."

"Did you take off that dog's head without me watching?" asked Boss Lady. "You never let me see the good stuff!"

I decided no answer was needed, called my dog and finally gained the peace of my car. As I left the drive the radio burst forth asking, "Did you forget the guy with the new foal? He says it's four-thirty and since you weren't there he wondered if you forgot that he has to go at five."

"Tell him to leave and I'll care for the foal alone. I won't get there before six."

"Okay," said Boss Lady. "Who's going to take the phone when I leave in a few minutes?"

****

CHAPTER FOUR

The constant problem was there before me. It seems that always, as I start on my late afternoon calls, the workers of the world, unconsciously programmed to the five o'clock whistle, begin fighting their way homeward to their television or their wives, or the customary beer at the corner pub, letting nothing get in their way. If a job needs finishing or the unexpected arrives they scream in agony and demand double time. My wife answered loyally through the beginning years and even made sure it was answered while she took a bath or went to the john but now the phone has become a monster. Her answer, now that she is bathed in comfort and security is, "Make some other arrangement. It's your business, not mine." Other members of this household that the phone supports are too busy to be tied down. My reluctant answer to Boss Lady----

"Give the phone number of the place where the foal is to the answering service. That's my last stop. They can call there." My clients don't like the service but I have no choice and it does do a good job.

In the now darkening evening I stepped from my car to greet Mr. Marlboro, the owner of the quarter-horse foals. He is a tall man but soft around the middle and is obviously a horseman of experience because he has a big silver buckle on his belt.

"Where ya' bin, for Chris'sake, Doc?" I'm a busy man. I took off from the plant early so's I could meet ya' and here ya' are late!"

Not wishing to explain the afternoon I said, "Hi, Ben. Where are the yearlings? You have some warm water?"

"I got 'em in a box stall," he said.

Inside the shelter I was greeted by two wild eyed young horses huddled in fear on the far side of a box stall.

"Put their halters on, Ben," I requested as I started mixing worm medicine and getting the stomach tube ready.

"Halters!" he said. "They ain't been touched in five months!"

My heart fell. A ten minute job would now take half an hour.

"I'm supposed to worm your horses, not break 'em for you," I said. "You know they should be halter broken within three weeks after they're born!"

"Well, I've seen you use a rope, Doc," he said, grinning. "I figured we can handle them."

My noose shot out in the stall spooking a couple of fear-ridden, spring-loaded young power plants. There was a crash of splintering wood as the colt without the noose cleared all but the top board of the gate and disappeared in the darkening gloom. The demon that I had noosed fought and screamed in fear, and as I slowly won I was changing my price schedule from piece work to hourly work.

In silence I "twitched" the little horse, passed a stomach tube, checking to watch its course down the esophagus by flashlight and then pumped in the worm medicine.

"Sure ya' got it in the right place? Did ya' skin 'im up any with that rope? Think the other one got hurt any?"

"Check 'em in the morning, Ben, "I said as I cleaned up. "And next time have those colts broke before you call. I'll do the other one when you get it broken."

"Okay," he said. "You sure can handle a horse!"

I was disgusted.

"That's the poorest way to handle a horse!" I said. "Start when they're babies and get rid of their fear so its not necessary to fight."

I noticed I was sweating as my big car moved through the evening mist and my thigh muscle began to pain and tighten where I had taken a strike from the colt's front foot. Ben had laughed and said something about almost getting hit where I lived but I missed the humor.

More coons were in my lights now as I ate up country roads and almost every half mile a rust colored bird flushed from the roadside. I smiled, recognizing the woodcocks pausing for night feeding on their long, lonesome trek south and admiring their ability to fly at night in trees and brush. This bird loves flat loamy places to probe for grubs and worms and can often be found in the night on country roads.

A series of small hills lay between me and the farm to the northwest where the new foal was. The movement of the front of the car up and over the sequence of rises stirred my memory of the bow of a ship in the darkened South Pacific carrying myself and fifteen hundred other acutely trained marines.

81

A lone male voice of a big Italian friend came over the ship's PA system accompanied by the guitar of "Lonesome Joe", another friend.

"If you were the only girl in the world and I were the only boy," coursed through the air softly in time with the rise and fall of the ship's bow. The romantic Italian voice savored every word and gave itself to the men who faced death and horror with the dawn. In the emotion laden silences between the stanzas, I, at eighteen, could feel the pulsating power of these superbly trained fighting men and could hear the mind-penetrating metallic clicks as weapons were checked and cleaned over and over again. In those dark moments with a starlit sky above, phosphorescent waves glittering in the sea below, we young ones were vibrating with power and confidence. I felt more a man and more alive than I knew possible. I have learned since that this is a thing to be recognized in all men and they should be diverted from the joy of battle and the energy channeled to the joy of living. People feel sorry now for young men going into battle and they should not. The young men are happy---feel sorry for those that love them and bought them plastic war toys as children. In all of us there is something that really loves swearing, drinking, fornicating without love, shouting, and killing. Our enemy is uncontrolled barbarism and those who foster it for power. Current periodicals give names to men of certain political beliefs as they scream slogans and brandish weapons. The Red Chinese, North Koreans, Murderers of My Lai, Egyptian-Israeli-Bangledesh guerillas------ -all should be left without name other than untamed barbarians, enemies of mankind. Many must die before education is spread wide enough for the lion to finally lie down with the lamb.

In this state of mind I saw the vivid flash of the sixteen inch guns as my landing craft passed close to booming battle wagons in the Pacific dawn and my heart was choking my throat. Actually, a car with strong lights topped the rise ahead coming at me and we missed a head on collision by one half second. In the minute or two following I turned over in my mind the vagaries of fate that had steered me from the paths of bullets, from the rending lacerations of shrapnel, and from lonely or lingering death in a far off land. With a shudder, then a shrug, I wondered how long my sojourn would be cradled on the breast of Lady Luck.

*****

A small light far up a hillside across a thirty acre pasture, bathed in slowly waltzing evening mists told me I was at the brood farm where the new foal and its mother waited. When finally my car came to a halt in the mud outside the small barn, the weight of the silence of the fields and hills around me announced that I was alone and could relish moments with my animal patients unencumbered with telephones and the usually unnecessary anxieties of worried owners. I was welcomed by soft nickering of other brood mares in the foaling barn. Beneath a heat lamp in the first box stall the new foal stood with its huge mother standing over it with fire in her eyes, her ears back, and her nostrils dilated. She was ready to do battle with this white clad

83

intruder. She came at me when I entered the stall but with a sharp command to "whoa" and a firm grasp on her halter she quieted recognizing my authority. I examined the foal for any abnormalities, gave it injections to ward off the death dealing infections that sometimes overwhelm new born animals, and examined its mucous membranes for the tell-tale signs of jaundice that indicate blood type incompatibility with its mother's milk. I examined the placenta left for me outside the stall to be certain that all of it had been delivered and also to note any signs of uterine disease in the mare that would be mirrored on the surface of that membrane. For a full ten minutes afterwards I sat on a hay bale watching the foal with its mother, now quietly and with pride, tending and talking to her new child. From other stalls I heard the stirrings of other foals and mares in waiting. Tiny droplets of mist drifted by the windows lighted to diamond quality by the barn lights. Beady-eyed mice scurried on well worn rafters and a cat moved fluidly across the bare floor like its jungle ancestors. This magic of the manger quietly impacts my soul and I bathe in its atmosphere. I am pleased at being even a small part of the wonder and thankful to understand it as well as I do for this was the very basis of the personal value that I felt now.

"KJW425," resounded from the night outside the barn and I recognized my wife's voice slightly irritated. I rushed outside scaring all the mares and breaking the spell within the barn. I started the car with the roar of modern machinery insulting the quiet and grabbed the hand microphone.

"I thought you weren't on the phone," I said thankful that she had been.

"There's some big guy in here with a hound full of porcupine quills and Mr. Bently would like you to see his old dog after your dinner sometime," she snapped. I knew she had taken the phone out of ingrained habit and was mad because people had interfered with her carefully planned dinner.

"I'll be in half an hour," I answered wearily.

****

CHAPTER FIVE; Monday Eve

The road down the same mountain I had traveled the night before was uncluttered for almost everyone was home having dinner. I walked into my office to be confronted by two clients who epitomized the diversity of my clientele. Mr. Bently, with long silver hair, and expensive suede fur lined coat, and a silk scarf inside an open necked shirt, sat with his fat cocker spaniel in one corner. He was trying not to notice Neil Porker chewing his cigar, dropping ashes on his red plaid hunting coat, and holding a dirty piece of rope tied hastily to a raw-boned coon hound whose face and mouth were full of porcupine quills.

"Looks like Spring is coming, Neil. The porkies are around again," I said. "C'mon in. It looks like Jake is in more trouble than old Bacchus there. Good evening, Mr. Bently."

"Yes," Mr. Bently said vaguely with a quick smile that I knew was practiced in the Après Ski bars in winter in Switzerland and the sun filled beaches of the Riviera. Neil stomped by into the surgery and when the door was shut he said, "Who's the creep with the lap dog?"

I smiled knowing his earthy but sequestered life had been spent within the confines of this valley.

"Oh, he's okay, Neil. Just different and worried about his dog like you are."

"That's a dog?" he grinned. "This here's a dawg, Doc, but pretty dumb tonight. He knows what a porcupine is. I'll help you knock him out agin and then go like usual. Guess you ain't got a pitchfork yet, have you?"

Mr. Porker was referring to the old timers practice of removing the center tine from a three tined hay fork and pinning a dog's neck to the ground to remove quills in the days before anesthesia.

Neil left after we knocked out old Jake, and I asked Mr. Bently in after moving the sleepy hound to another table.

"Old Bacchus hasn't been eating and he's not feeling well." the nervous Bently said.

Bacchus was overweight and physically, if not chronologically, old. He squinted at me through his wrinkled face and though spoiled, defensive, and overweight, I could see he was troubled. A brief examination revealed his malady.

"He'll have to lose a few of those teeth," I said. "I would suggest that we give him antibiotics and if you'll leave him I will get those teeth out tomorrow when his blood level of the drug is high."

"Oh, I couldn't leave him. He'd be heart-broken," said the polished champion of the cocktail circuit.

I respected his deep feeling for his dog and said, "Okay. I'll give him a shot and you bring him back at two o'clock tomorrow."

Mr. Bently mumbled something about missing the art show at the library but was happy with this solution. I gave the good old dog a good belt of penicillin and said goodnight to the beautiful gentleman.

Jake was snoring loudly as I lifted him to the surgery table and then started pulling quills. This job I knew would be repeated many times in the next few weeks. My eyes were tired and the last few quills hard to find, but I finally finished and placed Jake in the cage next to the terrier I had operated on earlier in the day. The reeking old coon dog next to the immaculate white champion terrier brought to mind again the differences in the clients that I contact in this hilly area, once remote but now only two and one half hours from a metropolis. The terrier's pulse was good and as I petted her, her eyes blinked and a vague wag came from her tail. I choked a bit thankfully and covered her for warmth.

Up in the kitchen my wife greeted me with a steaming plate of food which I consumed mechanically as I recounted the day.

"You must be tired," she said though she hadn't been listening. Take a shower and get some sleep."

"Well, tomorrow is Tuesday," I said. "I'll make it."

For five years now I had been taking off from Tuesday night to Wednesday night and seemed to be able to take any pressures by simply realizing that Tuesday night was coming. The previous ten years I had worked seven days a week parting with so much of my self that I scarcely knew what day it was or what sort of man I had become.

I came from the shower and was asleep in about five minutes when the phone jangled by my bed.

"I'm certainly glad to find you in at last," said a woman's voice. "Can I get my dog in the morning?"

This was the terrier's owner and I could see she still did not take her dog's surgery very seriously. I was glad the dog was alive and she wanted to get it home immediately.

"Well she seems okay, fortunately," I said, "but she'll have to stay until Friday or Saturday."

"She won't stand for that," said the lady, "and I can't afford it."

"Don't worry. We'll take good care of her and if you're strapped for money take a little longer to pay," I replied. "She has got to have professional care for a few days."

"Well, all right, but I'll call every day," the voice said.

"Fine! Good night, M'am."

I went to sleep thinking I should scare some of my clients more when things are serious, but which ones should I scare? The games professional people must play with the minds of mankind are sometimes bizarre when you try to be compassionate and calm their fears. The crux of the process is the care of my patients and I often give the owners too much credit for understanding.

Sleep was coming a little slower this time. The phone rang again.

"Doc," Tony said, "June's straining a little. Do you think she'll cast her withers?" (Evert her uterus or inside out.) "I'm really too tired to stay up and watch her. Four-thirty comes pretty early. She is up and eating though."

With a prayer and a calculated guess I said, "Tony, I think she is straining because she has a large closed cervix and my guess would be she won't evert her uterus. I'm pretty beat myself. Call real early if there is trouble!"

"Thanks, Doc. G'night."

I lay for a moment hearing my father's radio and my wife and daughter's television as their normal life went on. I would be wakened once more by my wife's retiring but could fight sleep no longer. Monday was over as far as I could tell.

****

CHAPTER SIX: Tuesday

"This old whore is driving me nuts. Why didn't you warn me about all this when I asked you about breeding Carol's mare?"

The weary, concerned voice came over my phone at four o'clock Tuesday morning. It was the dedicated father of a Four-H girl horse owner who had convinced her parents that her mare should be bred the previous April. Dad knew nothing about horses but, like many of his kind, stuck by his kids if he thought that what they were doing was good for them. He had attended all my illustrated lectures about mares and foals and now had sat up for five nights because the mare showed all the physical changes of imminent birth that I had documented.

"What's she doing, John?" I asked.

"The silly bitch just stands there for a while and then lies down and groans. I just don't know what's happening," he said with a worried tone.

"She's just crowded in that belly, John, and feeling damned uncomfortable. I wish it were possible to tell you when, but I can't. When I saw her Saturday she looked ready. She will lie down one time and that foal's feet will float up against the cervix and away she'll go. What's she doing now?"

"Standing there looking at the floor like a dumb drunk ape!" John said, his weariness and concern showing. He had installed a phone near the box stall for the maternity episode as I had asked because equine birth is so fast and violent that I often cannot get there in time. Many foals have been delivered over my phone just by giving directions based on immediate observations.

"Go get a cup of coffee. It's going to happen anyway, soon."

"Coffee! Jeez Christ I been livin' on the stuff. I'm so hopped up now I'm trippin' over my eyeballs and if I ever fall I'll drown in the two feet of pee I've put in this barn! It's so cold in here now I couldn't find it to pee with if I had ta."

I subdued my laugh over his state and said, "Well go get some hot cocoa and while you're in the house tie a string to your pecker---or better yet, get your wife to. Did the mare eat last night?"

"No," he said while chuckling. "She picks up hay and drops it all over. I'll go now. I'll call again. See ya', Doc."

Because of the remark about the hay I immediately thought 'that mare is going to foal before daylight' but could not be sure enough to tell him so. The call was one of the many that come this time of year from worried horse owners in the quiet hours of the night. Rarely is there trouble and over the years I have learned more about foaling mares by phone than any other way. I never discourage calling because I would rather be wakened than get a case too late. I returned to a fitful sleep worried about the mare but confident in John's conscientious care.

The phone clanged again and I saw the clock said six-fifteen. A quiet voice said, "It's here, Doctor. John wants to know what to do. He asked me to call. I'm sorry, it's so early!"

In the background I heard a young girl's voice say, "OOOOh, it hit the wall, Daddy. Is it hurt?"

Then a thud--then a curse--then, "jeez looka the blood--hold still you little shit. I'm trying to get this cup on your belly button."

"That's okay, Charlene. I gather that the baby has arrived and John is trying to disinfect the navel as I told him. Sounds like all is okay except John."

"Oh, yes, that's right," a calm, rested Charlene said. "John came down about four-fifteen and fell asleep. It was here when we both woke and came back to the barn just now."

In the background again, "The little bastard kicked me! Carol, you watch that friggin' horse. She looks like she'll kill me any minute."

"My horse wouldn't hurt anybody," pouted Carol.

"She already bit off half my ass, Girl. Do as I ask or I'm dead."

"Put John on the phone, Charlene. Things sound fine," I said.

"Yes, I'll get him," said the quiet voice.

"There's an awful lot of garbage hanging out of that mare, Doc. You comin' over?......Please."

"That's normal afterbirth," I said. "She'll drop it soon. Did you get the navel disinfected?"

"Yup," chuckled John. "I dipped his pecker three times before I realized where the umbilical cord was. No wonder he kicked me. His old lady's a bitch all of a sudden. Sure am glad it's over. I'm going to work to rest."

"I gather it was born while you were down for cocoa, " I said, knowing how often it happens.

"Yeah. I was cold and shook so I crawled in with the old lady for an hour or so. I'm gonna wake her up in the morning more often, Doc!" said the happy voice.

"Poor mare left alone to struggle through motherhood and you're down there playing hide the wienie with Charlene," I teased.

"But, Doc....I was beat. Awwwwwww, go to hell and then come over will ya'?"

Usually when inexperienced people are watching a foaling mare, every time she lies down a light snaps on and somebody looks at her so she gets up again removing the pelvic pressure necessary to start birth. When they leave for coffee, etc., the mare stays down long enough to start the process.

So started Tuesday. I had about ten hours before my day off started and I could consider my own rebirth.

The black haired girl I live with was in the john and soon headed toward the kitchen where her arrival was awaited by two small dogs and one huge cat, each of which tore at her compassionate nature with subtle ploys they had learned worked to give them food, drink, in, out, or petting. I had learned or rationalized that it was best to stay in bed at this time to answer the phone which rang often and always was for me. I savored this time specially to watch the comings and goings of the birds I have fed for years outside my huge bedroom window, and to note the arrival of new species, though they appear sometimes as new ethnic groups demanding welfare.

The phone rang and when I reached for it the movement startled all the birds to fly like bursting rockets from the snow-covered ground into the new shafts of sunlight.

"Doctor, I understand from the horse dealer that you are good with horses. We kind of think that the horse we bought at the auction last December could be pregnant. Would you come see? This is Mrs. Orvington in Childsville."

"Yes, Ma'm. I'll be there about ten this morning." I replied. The trick now was to build other calls around the two I had in order of geography and time. The phone rang again.

"Doctor, I have a cow I can't get with calf. Will you see her today? She's in heat!"

I made the geographical circle bigger but the time was okay. "I'll be there about nine, Mrs. Klavern," I said.

The next call was an excited lady who said her dog's eye was hurt and could I please see it right away. I told her I could see it on my way out at seven or at office hours at two PM.

"I would like you to see him about eight-thirty, Doctor," she said.

"I'll be taking calls on the road then, M'am. If you can't make it at seven-thirty it will have to wait until office hours."

"I didn't know you went out on calls, Doctor. Will you stop here?"

I only go out for horses and cattle or for dog owners who can't possibly come because they are crippled. I really can't do an adequate job on dogs at home."

"I didn't know you cared for farm animals. I've heard you are so good with dogs. Which do you like better?"

Knowing full well my answer to that would be carried from library meeting to coffee klatches for years I avoided it. "I'll see you at office hours, Mrs. Grograin. Good-bye."

"Mmmmmm, good-bye, Doctor."

Immediately the phone rang again.

"Parade horse has a nail 'nits foot. This is Steve. Can you handle it alone? I got to get to work."

"Sure, this morning, Steve. So long," I said happily realizing Steve's place fit my circular route. "Bye."

For brief moment I savored the utter comfort of pulling the blankets up to my nose feeling secure, isolated, and privately poised to deal with the hours ahead. There were cowbirds on the ground around the bird feeder, meaning Spring. The doves waited in the trees for the raucous starlings, jays, and grosbeaks to finish gorging themselves. The red squirrel flicked nervously out of the wall to grab a morsel while fearing the slashing dive of a sharp-shin hawk we both knew lived near. I lay there, my insides vibrant as a turbine fairly glowing with the prospects of a day of useful, observant, cognizant life ahead of me.

A hot shower, breakfast, setter dog let out, animals checked in the ward, and a note for Boss Lady to watch for Mr. Bentley's old dog, all took a whirlwind fifteen minutes. I was singing on my way to the new foal and my setter beside me stared straight out the window, embarrassed and confused by the sounds coming from her faultless master as he spun the big car through a sunny morning.

"While you were in the shower a guy called from up North to say his cow was going crazy and licking everything. Could you come right away? She can hardly stand."

It was my rapidly kissed and bottom-smacked wife on the radio not using call letters as usual and the ensuing conversation revealed another doctor's client had a scary case. I would go because my colleague had and would do the same for me. The detour really massacred my pat time and geographical schedule but this occurred almost daily. I increased my speed to try to keep time on my side and made the twenty miles in twenty minutes.

The cow was shaking and wobbly with snapping eyelids and had licked one leg to the point of bleeding.

"That's nervous acetonemia," I said as I proceeded with intravenous treatment. "She'll calm down in a few hours. If she's off the hook a bit tomorrow call your own Vet if he's back."

"You sure that's not poisoning, Doctor? My vet diagnosed lead poisoning a few years back and it sure looks the same."

His worried look expressed real concern and uneasiness with an untried, different doctor. I decided that being dogmatic, definite, and dictatorial would probably salve his immediate fears, would shorten my stay, and would assure that he would call his own veterinarian when he returned.

"Please, do as I say. I'm sure of the case and have seen many like it. I must go for I have many cases to cover in my own practice,"
I barked.

"Yes, of course," he smiled. "Would you please bill me?"

A very fine man I thought as my car sped towards my familiar hills and the new foal.

"KJW425," screeched a stressed Boss Lady.

"Here," I answered as my dog almost leapt from his seat.

"There is a lady here who says you'd be here at 8:30 to see her dog's eye. Where are ya?"

"Please tell her to leave her dog for me to see or come back at office hours," I replied.

"But she says she has to go to the drug store. She's upset with you," Boss Lady rasped.

Unable to calm myself long enough to pour oil on two seas I simply said, "Right, I'm signing off."

By then my car was parked at the new little barn housing the new foal at John and Charlene's before my mind could park anywhere.

Charlene had delicious coffee in the barn and the mare had "cleaned" or dropped her placenta. The young Carol stared with misty-eyed fascination at her new foal as it nursed, and John, fully recovered, stood proudly by his women, a champion and guardian. The sun was warm coming through the door and the moment was shimmering with emotional silence and booming with symphonic glory blaring the triumph of man and his family.

It was too much for me so, since all was well, I left amid profuse thanks for treating the little foal and apologies for early morning phone calls.

Mrs. Klavern's tiny farm was only six miles away and I arrived amid many barking dogs, chattering chickens, aloof cats sitting witch-like on roofs and beams, and an ever shifting flight of white doves. Inside the small neat barn I found six cows in stanchions. The young cow in the center straddled a saw horse placed beneath her belly ahead of her udder and shivered from the soaked state of her hind quarters.

"Hello there, Son," a quiet strong voice said.

I turned and a black clad Mrs. Klavern stepped from a darkened corner.

"The breeder just left. I think she'll catch this time. The moon's right---bull for sure, though."

"How come she's so wet and what's the saw-horse for?" I asked as I shut the small window behind the cow.

"I soaked her down with cold water to close her up after the breeder served her. The sawhorse will stay 'til tomorrow so's she doesn't lie down and lose what the breeder put in," she said casually.

"Oh!" I exclaimed as I pulled on my sleeve. It would do no good to explain that the breeder places semen inside the cervix and the cow couldn't lose it if she wanted to, nor to explain that conception takes place within an hour if all is right. Rectal exam revealed that the animal had not yet ovulated as evidenced by a firm follicle in the right ovary. I gave an injection to hasten ovulation and was thanked by Mrs. Klavern, who remarked again that the animal would conceive anyway because the signs were right.

"I haven't seen you for a year, Mrs. Klavern. I'm sorry but you don't look well. Are you ill?"

"Just recovering. Took a long time. Most people been gettin' over this bug in a week. I'm on my third week now. Everybody else gets round bugs, but I get square ones, ya' know," she said with a sly grin.

"What are you doing for it?" I asked with pretended intense medical interest. "Sulfur and molasses?"

"Nope," she replied seriously. "My mother made medicine out of maple syrup and turpentine. I still got some. Works great. It's good either internal or out-ternal!"

"That's interesting," I said and I was sure my mouth hung open at the uncorrectable misuse of words I understood very well. "I'll be seeing you."

The ride to Childsville cut through back country and included a road we all called the roller-coaster road because of a recurring series of hills and valleys. Each valley now held a burgeoning stream and each hilltop field harbored deer, even at this late your of the morning, searching for bits of green to take the place of the twigs they had lived on all winter. I turned in an asphalt driveway in the middle of a group of houses that all looked alike and manifested all the mistakes of environmental insult that man had made before. I thought of all the lakes I had seen from my

100

plane surrounded by closely packed bungalows and cottages like a necklace of death destroying the beauty man had come for.

Seven children of varying sizes piled around my car from behind the garage and peered at me and into my car as I got out.

"Where's your old plug of a horse with the fat belly?" I boomed. This brought lights of fun into the boys' eyes as the girls looked as if I had insulted their beloved father or lover. The mare apparently was a neighborhood project and each child held his own secret attachment to the horse deep within his soul.

"Out back, Sir," a bright eyed older girl said. "Oh, here comes Mom."

"Good morning, Mrs. Orpington," I said as I passed her standing on the back porch.

"Hi there, Doctor," she replied glistening with friendship and enjoyment of the situation - as I was also. "Coffee now or later?"

"Later, thanks. Where's the mare?"

"Out there," she motioned to a trim little shack in the yard. "You need help?" she asked as fear but resignation flickered in her eyes.

"Yep. Come on," I boomed conscious of the kids intense stares as they watched every move. I knew my casual air would give her confidence.

The mare was brought into the morning sun and I put the twitch on lightly amid quiet gasps then put on a sideline. The horse was obviously a focal point of neighborhood pride among the junior members as their various expressions - though different -

101

all added up to concern. I pulled on and lubricated my plastic sleeve and began reaching in to remove manure from the mare's colon to facilitate feeling the uterus. The expressions on the faces of the children kept changing like lights on a movie marquee as I secretly watched them knowing that this was the age group of bathroom jokes and puzzlement over sex. I always proceed boldly under the circumstances as I know from my own experience that it's better than hiding and the kids and their computer-like minds must be fed information.

All the faces were intense except a little red headed boy in the back of the circle whose squinty eyed look and screwed up face questioned my every move because he was smarter and was sure I was nothing but a quack pervert dressed in white who went around the country rectally insulting cows and horses.

"She's going to have a baby in about fifty days!" I announced. The effect on the circle of children was electric. The red-head's mouth dropped open, little girls reached for each other's hands, the older girl holding the horse brimmed over with quiet tears, two little boys smacked hands up on their cheeks, another older girl quietly bit her hand until she cried and mother fairly shone with knowledge of motherhood. This glowing moment, during which only I was composed and could take it all in, soon broke into a babble, "gee whiz" and "wow" from the girls to "I told you so!" from the boys. The redhead, trying to look nonchalant, silently skipped two or three times on his way back to the house for the cookies he knew would come with my coffee.

102

I could not, if I tried, describe the happy atmosphere around that table.

A conversation between Mrs. Orpington and the redhead caught my ear amidst the babble at the table, "But you really like your little sister, Mary, don't you, Keith?" asked a concerned Mrs. Orpington.

As fortune would have it at that moment a lull in conversation put parentheses around nine year old Red's cool answer.

"Oh yeah. But she farts too much!"

Mrs. Orpington looked pole-axed, the children giggled and I roared with laughter and said, hoping to calm things, "Well, everybody has different reasons for things."

A short time later I headed for my car with a child at each side holding my hands as if I were responsible for their happiness. In reality, they were responsible for mine. While driving away towards Steve's old broken down barn and the beautiful parade horse, a glance in the mirror showed a front yard filled with tumbling, wrestling children on their way to stare at the mare and wonder about the wee one living in the warm darkness of her belly.

The clock on the bank had said eleven-ten as I passed through Childsville and now I was moving past residences on the main road. I was listening to cross-talk on my radio and privately smiling at the conversation between a Midwest veterinarian and his assistant. The road turned and fell away ahead of me. In a flash I saw a child under two in diapers on the midline. I swerved

103

left, stopped, then backed and curled my car around the toddler. I opened my door and grabbed a hand full of wet diapers, then drove into a driveway to the left as a huge milk truck roared around the turn and small hill oblivious of his near slaughter.

The girl in the house was staring at the wall smoking a cigarette and consuming coffee when I came in carrying my reeking bundle.

"I almost killed your child, Ma'm. It was playing in the highway," I said handing her the child.

"*IT* is a girl," she said indignantly, "and I know you. You're the vet from up the line. They do say you drive fast. You should be more careful!"

"I drive well, Ma'm. If I didn't *IT* would be a pile of blood on the road. And I will call the baby IT until someone cares for it. Good-bye!"

My thoughts then returned to the ailing parade horse and a while later I turned into Steve's stony drive and up in back to the barn with a swift blast on my horn as I passed the house. I backed my car up to the barn, and as I was getting my bag from the trunk I glanced through my back window at the house in time to see a curtain fall as an observer retreated.

The horse inside the barn was standing in the stall. I backed him out with some difficulty and tied him to a post expecting someone to arrive to help at any moment. Steve had left the nail in his foot as I always advise people to do so that it can be removed and treated correctly according the depth it had penetrated. I cut out the hole, treated it with antibiotics, packed it with cotton, and was grateful for the horse's only rearing twice. No help from the low set, shingled house where the curtain had fallen.

I returned the animal to his stall and drove to the kitchen door. I knocked. A pink chenille bathrobe answered the door draped about a fat girl with pink plastic curlers in her hair.

"Oh, are you here? We'll be right out," she said with fake surprise. "Please come in."

"Two yapping dogs snapped at my heels and as they were being "disciplined" by being told they were "naughty" I was escorted into the living room which was, in reality, a hibernatorium for this plump structure and her suddenly active mother. My eyes took in the empty coffee cups, the cigarette butts, the well worn pillows reverently holding the shape of the two girls' ample behinds and I explained how to care for the horse.

"We're sorry we didn't hear you come or we would have helped," said Mommy.

I knew they had heard, knew they would not venture outside until Saturday when daughter would ride in glory in the parade while Dad, who works blindly all week, waited by the truck to take the horse that he really loved from the hands of the women he was supposed to love (and quietly wondered why he didn't.) The glory over, Dad would return to care for the horse before and after the work he automatically went to daily in order to feed, clothe, and insure the future of the "insurance collectors" who waited like demanding baby birds in the nest at home.

"Ask Steve to call me tonight, please," I requested.

"Yes. He really shouldn't leave nails around," was the reply from Mom while daughter nodded in automatic agreement.

I had gone ten miles before my mind could calm itself from fury; then my radio blared, "A man called Hatchet says his horse is wrong in the 'snotlocker' and could you stop? What's that, Doc?" Boss Lady asked.

"Anybody knows that's a nose. Call and tell him I'll be there in eight minutes," I said with a laugh.

"Okay. Mr. Bently brought in his dog and he said to take care nothing should go wrong."

"Yep!" I agreed with hope. I knew the dog had endocrine and circulatory problems but also was suffering severely from rotted pre-molars. The choice to use gas anesthesia I had made many times before and usually resulted in a happy dog and a pleased client.

Irish Hatchet's stable lay on an area of open fields and probably was the oldest stable for miles around. The people that frequented this place loved horses and held the man that ran it in some awe and his word was gospel.

Irish detached himself from a group of admiring ladies in riding attire and came close putting his hand on my shoulder and as he said things slyly in my ear, with gross attention to secrecy as is proper in old world horse dealing, saliva from his lips dripped on my shoulder and the ashes of his cigar fell in my overall breast pocket.

"I'm trying to sell, Lover," he drooled. "Tell the lady it will be okay in a week. We both know he will."

The appellation "lover" comes from my practice of often taking young girls on call with me. Irish always stood leering when I arrived to see what new bird was with me and was sure in his own mind, either from experience or jealousy, that I bedded them all down. I have always been conscious of people's thoughts on these lines but have no intention of traveling these miles consistently alone. Most people know the pleasure of sharing experiences they love with an appreciative audience and I have also found that there are as many opinions as to the architecture of morality as there are covering the colors of horses. As horsemen know, this is endless and has no final judge.

Mr. Hatchet led me to a stall and, after I had treated the horse for an upper respiratory infection that caused the big animal's nose to discharge great masses of yellow pus, I came out and told him that the animal would be okay in a few days and that I thought it was a fine horse.

Irish agreed but added, "his ass sure will be glad when his head's dead," which meant that he felt the horse's head was too big. He also said that his friend, Bill, had told him the same thing about the disease and since Bill had been a "chancre mechanic" (medic) in the Navy he must know. I was forced to listen awhile longer as Irish explained a new method he advocated of making love to a lady when she's on the horse trails and attired in boots and riding britches. I quietly said I admired his inventive mind, fought down the temptation to top it with a fabricated suggestion of my own, and then jumped in my car and headed for the office twenty miles away.

The course of my journey to the office took me over back roads where dairy farmers waved from the fields and for a few miles down a main highway where the drivers of the great milk tank trucks roared to the cities. Their great air horns blasted as they recognized my car and while waving I think of the white frothy liquid milk sloshing in the stainless steel and glass, and additions to and subtractions from its initially faultless composition, until it reaches the thirsty mouths of children.

I was at that moment passing the small, perfect, but unkempt barn of an attorney whose horses I care for and remembered the superb saddles and bridles thrown carelessly in a corner to mold and the well constructed horse stalls left uncleaned. In a day's time I have gone from this barn and others of new affluence to the many barns of kids who educate themselves at 4H meetings as to nutrition and general horsemanship. Their saddles and bridles, purchased at auctions for a hard earned twenty dollars, now abide, carefully shined and oiled, on make-shift racks. This community in which I work abounds in these inequities and my desire to even them out is almost, I finally realize, a dictator's philosophy doomed for defeat.

I smiled as I remembered the attorney's visit to Irish's to buy a horse because he had talked to a few people at horsy cocktail parties and had become an expert. I had overheard a knowing Irish saying to this "Nouveau Cheval" person as his horse walked out for inspection, "Yep, out of Wassaic by Van!"

The attorney gave a knowing nod of approval as he surveyed the animal parading before him. Irish's foxy eyes glittered and I fleetingly thought of the various causes of hernias because I was in my car about to burst my abdomen laughing. I knew what the attorney did not. "Wassaic" was the horse auction and "Van" referred to Irish's moldy truck.

The sun was shining through my windshield as I turned into the south-west headed now for a woods road...Members of the state road crew working on a culvert moved and shouted in a friendly way as they carried on their easy pace. The end results of their superb work that never smacks of frenzy are wondrous and I marvel at their expertise. I know many of them and listen in a friendly way to their complaints because I know we in free enterprise pay them an enviable retirement. One summer day, feeling specially jovial, I spotted a sign ahead "men working". A full crew lounged by the road side and I knew they awaited a road oil truck. I shifted into a low gear for a fast getaway and stopped by the sun-bathing group.

"There's a sign back there says 'men working'," I said.

All of them greeted me in their fashion and the one that stood said, "Yup, Doc, that's right. How are you?"

"Where do I find them?" I asked and quickly sped away. My mirror revealed a memorable group of the most diversified collection of obscene gestures I will probably ever witness.

I turned out of the woods road and started down the next slope of the valley in which I live. A tumbling stream of water ran along the roadside and my mind flashed back to a Marine Corps Compound. In the common bathroom or "head" was a galvanized metal trough containing a more regimented stream of water and having, every three feet or so for a total of thirty, a wooden seat upon which men could sit to care for normal body functions. In the hours of late dawn after breakfast this was the scene of a conference-like group of thirty men sitting together and talking as if no such thing as privacy ever existed. Every five minutes or so a larger gush of water would come through the trough and was a source of some humorous remarks. One morning a resourceful friend of mine who was later to help me move a whorehouse in China, returned from a liberty and wadded up a great floating raft of toilet tissue and, as the great flush came, lit fire to it and sent it on its merry way under thirty vulnerable men. We stepped back for a moment to watch the sequential machine-like leaping of the men as the peril flashed beneath them and then stepped quickly out of the crowd unseen to fall in laughter in our tent.

I was laughing now as my car arrived at the valley bottom. Humor subsided quickly as I saw a drowned squirrel in a wash at the stop sign and remembered how I felt in the early hours of the morning after the third day in the battle for Guam. Foxholes were filled with water and I felt like a cigarette butt in the men's urinal. Twenty yards away a friend lay in water, his white face staring at the sky and water running red over a small caliber bullet hole in his forehead. A sniper's bullet we hadn't heard in the early firefight had swiftly ended his life and he lay quietly as did the squirrel.

I had parked my car amid four cars in my drive and was in the process of retrieving dirty coveralls and masses of plastic disposable packaging from my trunk, when a man said from behind me, "Hello, Doctor. Any orders today?" It was a drug salesman and we walked together into the waiting room.

I checked the black board I use for listing items needed.

"I guess no orders today," I said and noticed Gwen was somewhat anxious to talk.

"See you in a month," he answered and quickly left, smiling at the waiting clients.

Good man, I thought as Gwen began to speak.

"Jeepers Jones called and said he had a sick bull that was getting worse and could you see it right away?"

Gwen knew I had paper work, office calls, and surgery to do before hitting the road again.

"Please get him on the phone," I said as I pulled on my white coat for office hours and went in to greet the first client. Mrs. Grograin approached me in the waiting room looking frowny and imperious.

"I'm very busy, Doctor! What can you tell me about my dog's eye? I certainly missed him on my walk this morning."

I was turning over in my mind the many interpretations of the word "busy" preparing to answer when the phone was lain gently on the sill indicating Gwen had gotten hold of "Jeepers".

"Pardon me, Mrs. Grograin. Hello, Jeepers. What's wrong?"

"Damn Brahma sicker'n hell this marnin' when we fed. Looks like a hell of a belly ache. Better come!" Jeepers said and then belched.

I looked at my waiting room filled with people. Jeepers came from a long line of men who mistrusted "veterinaries"

111

because, like Jeepers, they practically always called late and therefore got uniformly bad results. I also reflected upon his long history of very slow payment and said, "It will have to be after office hours and surgery, Jeepers. Why didn't you call this morning?"

"It'll be too late then, Doc. I didn't get into the house 'till now to call."

"Sorry," I said and he hung up, leaving a hole in the pit of my stomach.

Jeepers was the man who remarked after I had said his horses were too thin, "Well, we give 'em all the hay we can." My suggestion to cut down on the number of horses if he didn't have enough hay fell on deaf ears.

"Well, what about my little dog?" asked the impatient Mrs. Grograin.

The phone was ringing as I answered her and the people in the waiting room who had been listening to this lady's continuous and practiced monologue awaited my answer. I concluded that she had left the dog with Boss Lady though I didn't know and said, "You saw me come in, Ma'am. I haven't seen it yet!"

"You mean my dog's been waiting all morning for you? I never should have left him this morning!"

"I agree," I said. "Come in and we'll have a look."

At that moment Boss Lady burst from the ward carrying a little dog.

"Nothing wrong with this dog 'cept his third eyelid is swollen. He's been barking all morning. When's he goin' home?" Boss Lady shrilled, obviously tense.

"That's my dog. Let me have him. You're choking him," Mrs. Grograin announced.

"I wouldn't choke no dog!" Boss Lady snapped.

She had the pup on the table. I looked and explained that it would be okay with medication and if not, the surgical correction was simple.

Satisfied, Mrs. Grograin prepared to leave but stopped and said, "The method you suggested for training my dog by using a whistle and then giving him a doggie treat doesn't work."

"Why not, Ma'am?"

"Now when I use the whistle all the dogs in the area come too," she sighed.

"Do you feed them when you feed your dog?"

"Of course, I couldn't refuse. Could you?" she snorted.

I had no answer. Compassion again had taken its toll. Here, obviously was no animal person.

Mrs. Grograin left. I discharged a cat (an animal welfare patient) to a lady who had five stony-faced children with her obviously disciplined by a woman whose nerves were raw from money problems. I thought how much better things would have been had I spayed her a few years ago instead of her cat a few days ago.

Mr. Tamoshan came in chuckling as usual saying, "How are ya', Son? Like my new dog?"

He was one of those nattily dressed, mustached fellows always smiling, always wearing a brightly colored golfing fedora and collar pin under a plaid tie. His natty black poodle had an abscess in its leg tendons containing a large thorn that I found after searching a while with magnifying glasses.

"Thanks, Boy." he said. "You're looking great. See ya' again," and left, a bright, happy man that I see perhaps once every two years, yet he is my friend.

"I want to see that day sheet!" I demanded of Boss Lady before she could start her usual complaint about too much to do. I ignored her remarks and started walking through the ward checking off patients.

A Keeshond and brown and white dog boarding; an Irish Setter puppy boarding, but I knew it had hookworms; a little gray cat with possible fracture of the wrist; a dark calico to spay; a German Shepherd pup with a lacerated nose from a muskrat fight (fix that nose, Doc, she's headed for Madison Square Garden); a large Shepherd belonging to a relative to be killed because it was dangerous; a Dachshund with an external chest tumor to be removed; a Norwegian Elkhound in for a lab test for kidney function; two cats for castration and two for ear mite infestation; a Spaniel who had bitten a man's new wife and she insisted he be killed, (the dog's personality was bad or I would have disagreed); two strays brought in by the dog warden; Mr. Watson's five Pekes boarding for a day while he was in New York; Mr. Bentley's dog, Bacchus; and three cats suffering from cystitis.

I gave Bacchus a pre-anesthetic sedative by needle so I would not have to use so much barbiturate then did the same to the Dachshund and the pup with the lacerated nose. I examined the cats to make sure their bladders were empty. The inflamed bladders that they had were produced primarily by domestication. The cases are numerous following big snow storms, demonstrating the fact that their fastidious nature doesn't allow them to use soiled cat pans at home and they won't face the snow outside. The resulting accumulation of urine causes rather severe cystitis and many are lost. "Domestication diseases" are becoming more prevalent in veterinary medicine and domestication accidents are increasing also. I have had pet raccoons killed in dishwashers, pet kittens killed in clothes dryers, two horses caught in swimming pools, an Angus steer in a well, many dogs smashed by cars and the snowmobiles that I hate, one pony and five or six cows electrocuted, and a few who devoured light bulbs. The stories that the old animals must tell their youngsters about people must be bizarre indeed!

The main thought in my mind was to try to get all the jobs done and loose ends tied up, for tonight was Tuesday night and represented the time when I dropped away from listening to all the anxieties of my clients, my family, and my employees. Exhaustion, frustration, necessarily subdued sorrow, and mental aberrations all forgotten from Tuesday night to Wednesday night. It is looking forward to this day of true living as an individual that carries me through the really chaotic trials with which my week is filled. A few years ago I heard myself almost screaming as

115

I vented my tired mind at my family because they never knew what I considered living and they, applying their own standard, seemed to say, 'that's the way it is. You chose your job.' I knew then no one could provide for me but myself so, come what may, I declared twenty-four hours off weekly and have been a steadily happy man since.

The phone jolted me from my contemplations. It was a man asking to come in with a dog with a sore ear. Office hours were over, I was run over with work and I wanted to break free, but the dog was in trouble and if I refused, he would not be seen until Thursday. I agreed that he come in and then proceeded to surgery.

As I passed through the ward I was acutely aware of the large brown eyes of a hound type mongrel stray as she watched my every move. The look was adoring, hopeful, and down-right lascivious. Her ten days after advertising had been up two weeks ago and I was supposed to have put her to sleep. Putting strays to sleep is almost a daily occurrence and normally doesn't bother me because most are misfits and I'm glad to save them from laboratories; however, now and then a dog such as this works into my heart and I procrastinate hoping to find it a human. The two weeks I had kept her were subsidized by no one and after the first ten days paid by the town, the decision to kill is mine alone. I am closer to ulcers and my wallet is thinner as "Jezebel" stays on.

I moved through surgery with precision and dispatch mainly brought about by finally harnessing and directing the tense energy of Boss Lady so as to make use of the superb abilities she didn't know she had. I removed the tumor easily; the nose I

116

sutured delicately and aseptically so that no scar would remain; I spayed the little calico cat; I drew blood from the Elkhound and set up the chemical test; I removed some of Bacchus's horrendous teeth and pushed back gums, and administered antibiotics. I then castrated the two tom cats marveling at the thousands done by this crude stretching and breaking of spermatic arteries with no losses and breathing thanks that I was born in an era when anesthesia was efficient.

The phone rang and when I answered it I glanced at the clock; four-fifteen and soon I could break free of six nights and days of tensions and drive to the quiet seclusion of my cabin to read periodicals I never get near during the week, to eat according to my needs, not according to ceremony or time, to sleep sometimes feeling as it may in death through familiar noises of forest and rain-swollen stream, through freshly washed air and sparkling stars and moon to heaven, I presume.

"I know it's Tuesday and yo'r itchin' to go, Doctor," said a strong Polish voice with a mild edge of humor, "but I got this here caow with milk fever but not the reg'lar. I'd give her a bottle myself but she'll go sixteen hundred pounds and she's one of these eyelid snappers."

I knew exactly what he meant and I trusted this square hunk of animal man. All my colleagues had told me at various times at monthly meetings where we trade stories of personalities and dead-beats, of how miserable this man could be. I knew only humor, good judgment and a superior ability to raise animals. It

117

meant a thirty-five mile round trip before I could break loose but I said, "I'll be there, Edward."

"All right, ma Boy!" and the receiver clicked.

Boss Lady rasped, "C'mon, I gotta get goin'."

Guinevere was saying good-bye as she left with the mail and my wife was arriving home from work at a prep school.

"Get the cats with the bladder trouble and the ones with the ear mites, one at a time," I requested of Boss Lady.

"I'm comin', I'm comin'," she squealed.

We treated cats in silence for a while and as she went back for the last cat I answered the insistent phone.

"You know that mare you looked at last night that just foaled?" asked a voice.

"Yes. How are things?" I answered a little worried.

"She lay dead in her stall this noon."

Shocked, I gave instructions how to handle the orphan colt and then turned to face Boss Lady as she came from the ward carrying the last cat.

"Better have a look at that old dog belongin' to that rich bastard with the foreign car," she said. "He don't look right."

I went in and found Mr. Bentley's dog, Bacchus, that had been normal under anesthesia a half hour before, in the last throes of

ventricular fibrillation and watched helplessly as he died in less than fifty seconds before my eyes.

I finished the last cat and then called Mr. Bentley to jolt him with the unpleasant news. He was shocked and his bitter recounting at parties of my slipshod medicine for years afterwards revealed only his limited knowledge and my inability to transfer any to him.

The mare had died of a vein broken during delivery that caused her to slowly bleed to death internally with no symptoms to a medically untrained owner, and, of course, none at the time that I saw her the night before.

At four-forty-five I informed the answering service that I would be out of the office as usual from Tuesday night to Wednesday night. I would rather my family answer to reassure the people who support them, but they usually forego the responsibility.

Driving that Spring night back from the big cow at Edward's towards my cabin, and in spite of a week filled with triumphs big and small, I heard in the wind passing my window the lonely whinny of an orphan foal, and saw in my windshield the face of ole Bacchus, defiant, but finally yielding to kindness, and felt the pain in Mr. Bentley's heart. Memory of the large brown eyes of the special hound who watched me and waited to die came as I heard soft wind in my pine trees, and sorrow outflanked the bastions of my defense. Gratefully I let myself fall into that sequestered world of Tuesday to Wednesday night during which I must be remote from others and meet myself head on so that I can regroup to face the interplay of triumph and tragedy in my life as it starts again on Thursday morning.

****

119

CHAPTER SIX: Tuesday night to Wednesday night

My setter's paw was pressed with her weight on my neck as she stood over me growling at the foraging coons outside the window at my head. A barred owl hooted with weird resonance in the pines around me and I awakened refreshed by three hours sleep, but violently hungry. In a few moments I had a fire dancing in the tumbled fireplace outside, a frozen steak in the chimney smoke and a cold beer in my hand. I sat on a familiar worn log, listened to the stream frolic over the rocks and watched as small white clouds, lighted by reflected moonlight, rushed past the pious pine tops over my cabin. It was one in the morning and like a whispering, warming cloak moving as a weather front the familiar mantle of self-appraisal moved over me. My mind moved to the outside and watched the veterinarian enjoy his solitude and revel in his joy of simply being a successful animal in the world that seemed to change daily.

In the years past I had driven myself happily at such a pace that it began to register with vague but painful signs of illness. It was recognized by my doctor, told to my wife, who informed my friends who "understood" and kindly thought they would provide relaxation. With no time for thought I would drop from my work and in a flash would be at a party that had been planned for weeks or at an outing that had all the earmarks of last month's "Travel and Leisure" magazine. I would stand and laugh or carry on intense conversations on world or local issues. I was uneasy in the clothes I wore only to be judged by other people. These activities were of my body alone and created a dam through which the plaguing anxieties for children's lacerated pets, farmers' ill producing cattle, and horsemen's endangered mounts could not flow. The drama of a typical day would not leave my mind alone and constantly I would wonder, 'Did I do all I could for the one that died? Or am I doing all I can for this one in danger?' Only after many hours of solitude would these ingots of thought cease to clank and find their niches. It took years for me to recognize that the source of inner unrest was due to the fact that my desires in life, other than the professional facet, although simple, were not universally accepted as being of a relaxing nature. I learned that drinking beside pool or patio bore the same relationship to relaxation as prostitution does to loving. I learned that being without creating something, if only an original thought, was a vacuum that subtracted from the total of my life.

The maintenance of myself as a creature of value to others, as a buffer for their emotions, as a savior of their beloved, as an imagined bulwark against their fears, or as a lover absolutely requires a time of solitude when I can consult with myself about the vacillating forces that act upon us and about the vagaries of human thought. I would like to tell you of a few Tuesday nights that have gone before.

*****

TUESDAY NIGHT: June

The last phone call had been made to a lonely widow whose great wise retriever I had found to have secondary tumors in lung tissue and to whom I had hopefully promised life for the balance of the summer. My car had been fueled and loaded with dog, fly fishing gear, and the week's supply of reading material that I never get near. I headed north turning over in my mind the few warm invitations I had had for Tuesday night from people I am close to, but since I yearned to be alone for a few hours at whatever cost, I bore on to a glassy clear lake on a mountain top twenty-five miles away.

I walked in beside a client's cottage through hemlock and laurel now in bloom to a small wooden dock at the lake. There was a domineering silence draping the entire mountain range, and to the west, blue-black clouds built rapidly bringing a violent summer storm to rape the hours I had waited so long to use to try to fool a few trout into my creel. The nearness of the storm had put down the rise of fish that normally started at this hour and in the stillness that preceded it I could hear the swish of wind and rain advancing over the hardwood hills. The lake surface, as yet unruffled, reflected the sky-bound lightening and my dog drew near me worried as the holocaust approached. A fierce bolt of fire slashed into the forest nearby and I moved to the safety of the house.

The storm came on, whirling the great hemlocks into a desperate dance. The lake churned, lightning flashed, rain and hail pelted the water as its surface heaved in the darkness. Leaves and small branches sailed upwards in the many small winds that made up the storm. The darkness that came with the onslaught was charged with electricity and the flashes brought me back, without fear, to a crazed and saki-driven "banzai" charge of enemy troops in the night on a ravaged Pacific island. We shot rapidly at figures silhouetted in flashes of explosives and star-shells sent in answer to our radio plea to ships lying off the coast.

The storm left a peace both in my mind and in the magic summer evening around me. Across the deserted lake scattered whirlwinds now carrying mist rose up in the forest and moved through it like a few maniacal huns left behind a war party to proceed with their residual gleeful killing. Relentlessly, life began where it left off. Birds began to converse, tentatively at first, then joyfully announcing approval of a well washed world. Nymphs rose from the mossy submerged boulders in the now settling but rocking lake to hatch on its surface and release large winged May Flies for their once-a-year appointment with brief courtship, mating, and egg laying, thus assuring the repetition of the cycle next year. My setter, feeling peace now as did I, stared off at the distant wooded hills thoroughly absorbed in the pulsing silence. She jumped and looked at me in question as trout began to rise noisily on the gently heaving surface, and then she ushered into shore the two that I caught easily in the next ten minutes. By lantern I cleaned them on the lake's edge, leaving the offal on

123

shore for the raccoons that night. My treasured knife slipped off the rock shore and as I reached for it among the multicolored boulders, I could feel the soft coolness of the lake water on my arm. I stripped and swam strongly through the dark water that flowed over my body now surging with animal power and freedom, then returned to my cabin to sleep refreshed and fulfilled by facing the natural world alone.

Sometime during the sequestered privacy of that fresh cool night a lithe brown-haired girl slipped quietly unafraid through the pines, whisked deftly into my sleeping bag and clasped her nude body to mine. I was expecting words of love but she whispered, "I picked up some beautiful stones for that chimney you're building. They're in the car."

In the pine scented dark I smiled and the love that followed grew in intensity as did the earlier storm and left the same silent peace as we slept.

*****

TUESDAY NIGHT: October

At a diagonal to the runway's center line ran the even edge of a shadow cast by a mountain in the pinkish light of the setting sun. Flashes of orange fire flickered in the windshield from the turning propeller's reflections of the sun and they moved into me as the rhythm of music is felt. My eyes moved slowly from gauge to gauge on the fire-wall, carefully checking fuel, manifold pressure, rpm drop and recovery, oil pressure, vacuum pressure, engine

124

heat, altimeter, carburetor heat, while my hands and feet checked the freedom of control surfaces. I tested the radio transmitter and receiver by calling the airport office to check out for an hour's local flight.

Shortly before, I had called a halt to practice because I was wrung out and tense from carrying many emotions for six days before. Days in my profession are twenty four hours of attention, not the eight hours work that so many consider a day. I am pleased that I enjoy my work to the degree that extended hours don't bother me and I don't feel pressed because I must squeeze a day's work into eight hours. My last act that evening was to lift the limp, broken body of an impeccable German Pointer from the trunk of an old couple's car. They had hit the pup and the anguish in their eyes was matched only by the bitter hopeless look on the face of a sixteen year old boy standing with crutches beside his own car at my office. He had called me a few weeks before to ask how he should start training his new puppy for grouse work. I turned, empty, and as the people silently left carried the body into my office, my own tears falling into the mangled mass that had been the puppy's head. Within minutes I was packed and headed for the airport, thankful it was Tuesday night.

Vibrant power came through my hands and feet reminding me to change to finger tip control and gentle toe pressure. The lift off came and I rose from evening into sunlight, from earth-bound shuffling to buoyant freedom, from a constant headwind of human emotions to the exalted joy of being totally alone with my capabilities. I learned to fly in order to turn a fluctuating animal instinct that carries me so well in medicine into a disciplined, pre-thinking machine. Only in flight alone was my safety due entirely to my own skill, and it occupied my mind enough to put all other problems aside.

I trimmed the little plane to eighty miles per hour and climbed gloriously to eight thousand feet. I spent the next hour rolling over silver clouds, turning up to watch a setting sun and a rising moon, flitting briefly through shadowed familiar valleys, following silver streams at treetop level, and watching with pity as lights came on and the masses of people became entrapped by television sets, hamburger stands, outdoor movies, and bowling alleys. My mind was clearing now in its structured role. My radios gave me a point of location and within minutes I slowed my engines, flicked on landing lights, and descended slowly through still evening air to land softly on the runway nestled beneath the mountain that bore my name. Within an hour the moonlit pine forest, the whisper of moving water, my magic cabin and the quiet brown-haired girl held me within their common embrace.

*****

TUESDAY NIGHT: August

I had finished late that evening in a farm kitchen where a ritual had taken me. A number of the farms that I am called to care for are run by the sons of immigrants. The younger generation faces closer margins of profit, high machinery costs, new state regulations that demand new sewers, milk room equipment, and much pressure to increase efficiency while the parents, as in the old country, demand respect and still control the purse strings. It is an unspoken rule that a man who performs a service is paid immediately, but to collect he must sit with the patriarch and break bread with him. Sometimes it is old country "Schnapps" (deadly). This evening it had been delicious cake and unequaled coffee and the two cups I had hungrily consumed now exacted their caffeine toll.

Many miles after I had left the farm I had parked my car and walked off into the night. My course over the wooded hills and through dew-laden meadows was unplanned, I think, and my mental efforts to quell the anxious pulse of responsibilities of the week took place over considerable territory. Each sound, each smell, each scurrying animal was familiar as it came and went and by now, as I rested in a birch grove on a hillside, the full moon had risen and its light, sifting with an imagined tumbling sound through the light ground fog, gave birth to the magic light known to country people as "moon-glow". From the swamp lowlands came the deafening chorus of frogs singing of their joy with the soft evening given them now for the happy business of living. In the meadow in which I walked were a doe and twin fawns but my passing was down wind and their movement at the sight of me in the moonlight brought a chuckle to my throat, because without a scent they really didn't believe that "man" was walking about at such an hour. Through the misty night that held only the fears of people unfamiliar with an animal world I walked to a darkened house - to suntanned arms, soft brown hair, to a person of warmth who listened - who loved - who lulled me to a gentle, welcome sleep.

*****

TUESDAY NIGHT: January

I pretended the trip across the wind-blasted snow laden driveway was a brief segment of a journey in Siberia and I was a savior of a political revolution delivering a vital message to the soon to be leader of masses who was in reality myself. This flitting of my thoughts did very little to divert my mind from the fact that I was cold to the bone and the day's work in cold barns, I was sure, had produced the lacy frosted images seen on winter windows now upon the surface of my liver.

Instead of seeing a warm fire I was invited to make one as I came into the warmth of the home I had built and I turned back out into the biting wind to fetch wood. In brushing the soft snow from the woodpile I decided that once a fire was built for my family, snow or not, I would head for the inn to the north where food and grog and multiple gleaming fireplaces awaited the traveler. If I told my family of the cow I was trying to save that day..told of her everted uterus frozen to the barn floor that morning, or of the horse that fell through the ice of a farm pond, or of the splendid Abyssinian cat in for cesarean section that afternoon, I would be immediately suspect of complaining instead of wanting to pour out the tales that held me in manacles of tension. This was my conclusion, not theirs.

128

The doors to the inn, ten feet high, imported from some old land, gleamed in the light of a copper lantern in the entrance way. From up the stairs ahead of me I heard a few people laugh and my entrance was recognized with a few brief "Hi, Docs" from a few men I had met here before as we all escaped for a while from the demanding professions. This night, in front of a fireplace built of stone a hundred years before, I sat for two hours in an atmosphere uncluttered by the nervous radiations of competing women to listen to stories from a man just returned from Madagascar, from a retired ski instructor from Austria, from an English professor at a nearby preparatory school and from a race driver in his forties just returned from Baja, California, to see later that night a permanent girl friend who lived in the New England hills. They in turn listened with warm interest to a veterinarian, happy in a general rural practice and who cited memories of Pacific and Caribbean Isles, of horses and dogs and women he loved, and of the land that he knew so well.

The small light on the Inn's sign lighted the whorls of snow as they spun around the sign post. Through the window of glass, old enough to distort the image, I saw the sign's paint was cracking and felt such a sated peace in this solitary retreat that now body fatigue came over me. I bid good-bye to the stellar group and drove a few miles through the snow to a resort in the hollow of the foot hills where the woman at the desk in the old converted barn nodded to me and bid me sleep well. I stood for a moment in front of an eight foot fireplace and stared into coals that had burned for many days, then turned and found my way to a warm bed and slept deeply away from the twenty four hour problems that fill six days and nights a week at home.

****

CHAPTER SEVEN: Tuesday night/Wednesday morning. The present.

It was two AM Wednesday morning and the memory of previous Tuesday nights had taken but twenty minutes. Now, in mid-week as in mid-life, I found I was deeply troubled by being divorced by my wife of twenty-five years.

Though I did not initiate the process, I had considered it a few years before because of wide philosophical differences between us but took no action because of being involved sixty plus hours a week in my practice and because my children were young. In addition, my mind was knocked way off track by the disorienting problem of falling out of love---a great deal more puzzling than falling in love, I found. Currently my kids were fine but should I feel sorry for making a decent lady feel unsure while I felt empty because she lacked the capacity to help me face the toll my busy world took on me? Also, as those things go, by this time the brown haired lady saw strength in my love of life, saw my anxiety from time to time, and she listened--she listened and argued for twelve more years until we stopped for lunch one day and married.

The emotional puzzles in my life, the only ones, began one day when I was made to realize that all the equity I had worked for all my working life could be blocked from my use on the whim of my ex-wife whom I had shielded from work pressures (reality) for twenty years. A screen lit up in my mind flashing "MISTAKE!" and I knew I must start all over again to build equity I could use.

The fire-house talk at the time wove tales of all the young girls that rode with me. I knew of the talk but considered it normal human gossip and desired to decide about my life and not leave it up to the "Mr. and Mrs. Joe Sixpacks" of the world. Some of those girls now help make up about sixty percent of my profession and I relish the time spent with them--though these relationships were not of the glowing, lascivious style people talked of. The talk effected my wife but those were a great deal longer than eight hour days and left no time for sexual games. Besides, they were all too young.

Surrounding me in the night were the subtle communications of the night creatures. I could identify them all but could not delineate things amiss in my marriage. My ever working spouse seemed to fear the hundreds of people who made up my life and did not seem to care to hear of the strong emotional anxiety and extraordinary happiness that each day brought. I have since watched my children change in wondrous ways but my wife clings to the same philosophies she has clung to for years. It became obvious she clung also to decorations, cars and clothes.

It became obvious also that I had killed the love of my wartime sweetheart by blustering caffeine-fueled dominance of her life in an attempt to make her feel protected and secure. The vision I held in mind after papers were served was of an irate Goshawk with wings around all our belongings, driven by fear of the unknown, screeching "get out".

I knew I would gain nothing in courts because situations like philosophical wasteland and emotional vacuum do not exist in legal parlance. They know only "marital breakdown" and "adultery" that often follows. I also knew that there would be no nest-egg for later years and I must double my efforts at a time when I should slow down somewhat. A large financial saving was my knowledge of drugs and I could handle the final diagnosis not with endless insurance payments but with the quiet, self-induced euthanasia I was so familiar with. The wise lady I eventually married understood this.

That starlit night I will not forget--I overcame the only anguish in my life and went onward against mid-life a stronger, happier man. Tomorrows were mine to enjoy under my control. My animal work was my happiness and my art. My strength and joy was my knowledge of the natural world and no one could take away what I really was.

A buried problem surmounted, I returned to my sleeping bag and, sleepless still, I picked up the only book nearby. It chronicled the Pacific Was and place after place and name after name leapt from the pages to deal a shattering moment of tears as a suppressed memory awoke. From age eighteen to twenty-one my senses had taken in incredible scenes and valor beyond description. I had lived with Marines, Sea-bees, Sailors, Aussies, New Zealanders, and indispensable coast watchers. The air was filled with George Bushes and the seas with Jack Kennedys. I remembered so many things my mind had not yet processed, and my intellect, broader now than then, saw, as the full picture was developed, the position we held in the history of man.

I thought of the lovely villages of northern Okinawa. How, I had wondered in those days, could the culture we opposed have spawned these gentle people and quiet gardens as well as the bestial Samurai that now defended the southern part of the island. With lethal tenacity they clung to Shuri Castle, Sugar Loaf, and the destroyed Naha City, their backs to the sea.

We controlled that sea and a solid line across the island. I thought we only had to hold the line and wait for surrender; but, we were hurled, driven by tradition I suppose, against hills of rock and endless fearsome caves. This day still finds my mind unable to really cope with that loss of good men and boys in a seemingly senseless slaughter. In my mind today a truck wallows past me in a misty dawn with bodies of young men piled in a cold bloody mass like cord wood. No body bags in those days.

In the Mariannas parents and children leaped from cliffs ahead of our fast entrapment of troops on a peninsula only because of their leaders' beliefs in propaganda.

The hour of landing on Guam: Bullets tear out the back of the Corporal I followed by ten feet. He had made the mistake of pointing the way as we ran with combat telephone wire. The Nambu machine gun was hidden in an embankment fifty yards away and only risked discovery to kill those appearing to be in command. I lay face down in jungle mud, formulated that hypothesis then left, speed fueled by terror, and finished the mission. I did not point and prayed all the way that I did not appear to be worth a bullet from hiding.

I had never talked of these things, and many others, not because of some hidden damage to my mind but because I knew that a man within a few yards of me could have a war tenfold worse than mine but I'd never know it. I am deeply puzzled that I had no trouble about the killing. I do know that more people with that reasoning should be in our political framework. They could use some truth...

Given the above, augmented many times in many places, can the reader possibly think for a moment of the relief--the rapturous release from years of fear that the next landing would tear your limbs off--that finally lighted the very souls of thousands of fighting men on the day the news came of the atomic bomb? A powerful move that saved untold millions of lives because we did not have to invade Japan. They would have savagely defended their homeland to the last child--and Marine. I am indeed proud of my country that it never used it again. I am indeed joyful we could spare the people and the beauty that is Japanese culture.

My enjoyment of the sights and sounds and the understanding of many of the mysterious ways of the planet, its creatures, and the taste of fresh water and birch twigs, leaves fulfillment and confidence within me. There is a lingering wonder if I was supposed to teach these things to my children, now disbursed, deeply loved, and way above average. I assumed they were as enchanted as I and the slow discovery that their sense of value proceeded on different courses (equally valuable) left me stupidly puzzled.

My daughter, moving with decisive confidence, married a witty, athletic man she knew she loved, and she has not had a time in her life since then that she was not cared for by this man to whom I will always be grateful. She is loved and admired by us both, and has far greater stature than my clumsy efforts can convince her of.

My son was dealt blow after blow as he matured. If not poorly timed illness it was accident, reproductive or vehicular. I longed to help with his hormonal head-on with the ladies but it was at the time when that gender was listening to unsure feminist leaders and in the blizzard of thrown away bras and misunderstandings, I could not help. My life was so simple. While I took out the garbage my wife made breakfast. I produced money, my wife produced a home. There was pride inherent in both jobs. Since those days my son has performed with grace and real humor.

I went out again beneath my beloved moonlit hemlocks, entranced by the moonlit musical stream and pondered the familiar life that continued beneath its softly singing surface.

A shape formed from a tumble of water and walked a sparkling riffle. The otter paused with one paw lifted and, feeling my presence, lifted her nose to locate the cause of her unrest. Failing, she left pretending to be busy and headed for a trout-pool we both knew down river.

An otter out now signaled the approach of dawn and I turned back to my cabin. The memories, the facing of buried emotions, ambiance of the night, beer, and solitude had sublimated many concerns and I cried freely with copious tears for the first time since childhood. They were generated from having finally the time for objectivity and the pervasive rapture of knowing I had become the person I always wanted to be.

I hoped then that the brown-haired woman and I would learn to love. It took ten more years but sleep only took ten more minutes.

****

CHAPTER EIGHT: Wednesday morning

A sex-crazed cardinal screeched me awake and my work ethic mind began to invent some productive thing to be done that day that I owned. Experience had taught me that you will get no help and you must cure yourself of the habit that says work must be done.

A tunnel of early morning mist lay ahead and in its frame stood two deer appearing suspended by two huge ears apiece, curiously watching my progress as my horse carried me at a lazy walk down a woods road. I wished to tell them I was an animal person and of my pleasure at their presence at this hour. However, ears twitching, heads trying for a scent, feet stomping, they became ghostly white tails fading in the mist over a tumbled wall. I laughed at the vision of me in their minds, of a strange looking animal, 'too big, too slow, a hump in his back...wind's wrong...let's go...yeah!'

When I turned through the gate on the path to the wooded reservoir, an urgent signal shuddered from my horse to me through my legs and I knew he felt life as I did that hour. A late spring storm had felled many trees a few weeks before and I had been through to pile them into jumps. I collected the big chestnut animal into a semblance of "control". He danced through brush and almost careened off the small bridge in his anxiety to go. I just about put him together again before he cleared the big hemlock with feet to spare, turned into the woods and careened

138

around a fallen tree. I dismounted and walked over the stream bridge leading a dynamo. I remounted and we flew down the pine bordered trail clearing jump after jump until he slowed where water pooled in a deep moss bed beside the path.

I was watching the sky reflection in the pool and examining the many gelatinous masses left by various amphibians when my setter hit the water at full speed and lay there drinking and panting. She glanced up at me and almost spoke of the contentment we both felt. I finally had learned that a man must discover where happiness lies and then gain it for himself. No other person, no matter how close, can know what makes one's life complete..nor will any one else worry about it very much.

Through the forest ahead I heard the cries of the water-fowl I had come to see for I knew of the territorial battles and mating contentions that would be in full swing this month. At an extended trot my wonder horse sped down the trail until, on my left, a favorite sunlit swamp appeared as a lighted stage in the dark hemlock grove. Brown and honey colored grasses reflected the morning sun and tannin-stained water twisted slowly through and laced itself around huge dead trees that gazed at me like old monarchs disturbed in serious thinking about their kingdoms.

My setter stepped in a bog and a pair of Mallards sprang to the air and further away a pair of Canada Geese lay their necks flat on the water near a great uprooted tree and were totally immobile. I smiled at their complete deception of the dog and continued more flying jumps down the tunnel-like trail until I broke into brilliant sunlight highlighting the graceful dancing of mist on the reservoir's lazily waving dark surface.

At the junction of the big water and the woodland stream an otter gamboled in the shallows gaily catching frogs and fish and munching them up gleefully.

This animal carefully analyzed my mounted profile and decided I was harmless. The Mergansers fishing doggedly in the dark water and the Osprey circling above were unperturbed at my presence (eating time) as I trotted my happy horse down the grassy road at the water's edge. In a moment I was conscious of a closely following wake in the water, fortunately just behind the peripheral vision of my steed. A large beaver, protective of his lodge and family nearby, was escorting whatever I was to where ever else he could. I carefully urged my mount into a faster trot because if our escort came into his field of vision my secure seat would be severely challenged by the initial curiosity of the horse and the resounding tail slap of the beaver. I was successful for all of twenty yards.

In that pregnant moment I recalled Murphy and his pervasive laws. This one covered a horse fly that made my horse turn to his shoulder (beaver-side, of course). He turned further to ogle the beaver, leaped in the air and pivoted as the tail popped on the water. Re-pivoting to leave the scene, my horse, overwhelmed with courage, broke my grip on the saddle and with a less than graceful arc I joined the beaver in the misty cold waters.

I surfaced to see my dog up to her shoulder at the water's edge, sorely puzzled about my activity. Down the road my horse watched in the same mind frame as the dog. I will remember forever the scene. In a huge dead oak over the horse stood three blue herons, an adult and two teens, watching the whole performance most solemnly and, I'm sure, wondering how man ever got to be in charge. Actually, the beaver was in charge of all. I whooped with cold and happy laughter and my dog preceded me to join my nostril-flared, snorting horse. The easy going herons left on wings with soothing strokes, no doubt in search of ambiance of a wiser and saner nature.

Later, in the saddle again watching the big waters and warmed by the morning sun, I felt fulfillment regarding my life that men are rarely privileged to feel. I have felt that way since, always when alone on mountain tops, on Caribbean Islands, in trout streams, and always when I have saved an animal and watched it rejoin its peers or anxious owners. I feel it when witnessing extraordinary performance by animals including man, or catching an admiring or grateful glance from a patient or his friend.

I walked back to the barn and the journey through hardwood forest was quiet and peaceful as were most Wednesdays in my life. I looked forward to brushing and cooling my horse as I had been taught by the owners of the barn he lived in, a family of good people that loved an animal oriented life as I did and had introduced me to many traditional pastimes that I had only read about. I was grateful to them and pleased to work for them, but none were there this day. I was disappointed but, as things turned out, very fortunate.

I returned about high noon to my cabin, ate two priceless pieces of pizza from the ice-box and collapsed on my red wicker couch that was covered with a luxuriant winter pelt from a horse, I was told, named Maudie, then pulled a light cotton blanket over me and fell into a deep sleep in my pine scented, shaded, and silent hide-a-way...

My eyes snapped open and the declination of the sun told me hours had passed. My senses said I was being watched and I turned quickly over. A blond fair skinned girl stood beside me dressed in brief panties and one of my shirts, unbuttoned.

"I know it's your alone day," she said, "but my body said I should come. I hope I can climb in with you."

For emphasis the fingertips of each hand moved in slow circles over her pink nipples. She really didn't know it, but this girl awoke in me every carnal avenue my mind had ever known (and a few it hadn't). Under my hands and lips she had always become a pulsating animal form in record time. I threw off the covers, probably growling, and that wondrous lascivious creature clasped my body like it had grown there. When I wasn't involved with her breasts I could clearly recall minute details of the classically beautiful skin of her thighs as she was astride my body. Though she did not appear to move I felt as if I were floating in a gently swelling and receding shining sea. We both were happy with my knowledge of physiology, and specially anatomy, none of which my lips missed.

Two hours later I fixed her a steak and a beer and kissed her off to her job at the club. I crashed for nine more hours and woke powerfully equipped to face anything my unpredictable life could bring me. The memory of that truly natural girl has never lift me though now I love the brown-haired lady more than life itself. I hope she has memories of her own but I don't ask.

****

CHAPTER NINE: Thursday

There was a persistent slow drumming coming from inside the horse trailer as it lay on its side in the road amidst whirling lights and anxious men. I crawled into the upper or second stall to evaluate the horse's condition as his hooves steadily struck at the narrow portion between us. When I was far enough forward I looked down into a large equine eyeball that joined mine in a communion of fear and wonder of our joint enterprise. As I calmed him by voice and familiar stroking he relaxed and his eyes began to express, 'Jeez, Doc. Get me out! The things a decent horse has to do just to get to eat twice a day!'

Classic anthropomorphism, you say, but there was a change in the eyes, and I knew the horse.

I had called in at first light, after a short run with my dog, and had gotten word of the above problem. I knew the turn in the road, the animal, and just about all the people in a small town twenty miles to the south. In my concern for the terror of the horse, the people's concern, and the real danger on the misty road, especially to the new wave of urban oriented drivers, I flew through familiar country and arrived in about twenty minutes. The first selectman and the fire chief had total control and the resident state trooper stepped out of a blinking cruiser showing a classic and radiant shit-eating grin generated by full knowledge of what my speed had to have been.

With thick cotton rope, which I always carry, I threw a double loop on the two hind limbs and turned to tell those wondrous country men of my plan.

"I'm going to give the horse an injection in his jugular to knock him silly---please, when I say okay, not before, pull slow and steady. You will get no resistance, but don't jerk his legs off."

With that I crawled again into the upper stall and, more by instinct then vision, injected the beast with a curare-like substance and watched certain signs for complete relaxation.

Then I said, "DOIT DOIT!"

The horse disappeared from beneath me like speedy eerie magic and a cheer went up from a relieved congregation. I came out and, in a blink, the men flipped the trailer and had it off the road. They turned happily, problem solved, right? But there in the road lay twelve hundred pounds of paralyzed horse and in my face was a cigar stub attached to the growling countenance of the selectman.

"Just how long is that friggin' meat going to be in that shape?" came from the side of the cigar stub.

"Ken, give me seven point two minutes on your watch and that will be it," I answered.

Having dispensed with an aggressive boss type that I greatly admired, I watched the horse recover and with the boss's seven point two grunt I gave the equine butt a boot and the great horse was up in a flash eating grass by the roadside. Security, not hunger.

A car pulled up and out of the mist came three country women carrying coffee and home baked sugar buns for all. These

145

women, who would never think of not doing this as their men get out to act on anything, have been our bulwark and strength for generations. They are hard to find now and I miss them badly. To me they have been partners since the pioneers and their definition as women wanders now in uncertain feminist change.

Mention of coffee brings to my mind one of my favorite times ever that was happily repeated often and it usually occurred at this hour. Milking is over, the barn scraped down, kids on the school bus and I am asked in for coffee after working in the animal shed or barn. Though the caffeine probably caused more trouble to me than I know, the coffee was sinfully perfect. The farm ladies had many formulae involving egg shells or grains for this perfection but the common fact was that it was always the freshly made second pot of the day. It was accompanied by their best baked goods (the vet was there, and the chores were well in hand.) The humor and the country wisdom encountered then is a valuable memory and I hope they know of my love and admiration. I liked the cold toast the kids had left more than the baked stuff and recall how I liked the way the farm butter showed up in that coffee as I dunked. A cardiologist's bad dream, but I felt fine at the moment.

However, there in the road a large strongly built man stepped from the bunch around the women. This was Emmett who, with his brother, ran a superb dairy farm a mile away. They had a combination of Yankee shrewdness, traditional love of animals and land, and brains, all of which made calls there a pleasure..whether on brutally hot summer days or on frigid mornings before dawn.

146

"I won't bother you now, Doc," he said, but we have a few calves to vaccinate when you have time."

He referred to vaccination of female calves against brucellosis, a contagious abortion causing disease known to humans as "undulant fever".

"Are you behind in the chores because of this emergency?", I asked.

"It's okay," he said simply so we decided to act now as I was here and needed the barn phone anyway. In ten minutes we were in a deeply bedded stall rounding up good looking calves.

Emmett held the calves as I juggled a lethal vaccine syringe, ear-tags, tagging pliers, ink bottle, and tattooing pliers in busy hands and coverall pockets. Emmett's brother holding the next calf laconically said, "If you had a broom up your butt you could sweep the barn while you're at it."

Stories were exchanged involving injecting or tattooing oneself but I assured them I hadn't aborted yet anyway. The job finished, I headed for the phone to find what the day held in store added to what I already knew.

"Joe Banko's still holding that mean blue cow in a wooden stanchion for you. He says you're half an hour late," screeched Boss Lady on the phone, "and again I got no cage for that Jezebel hound that loves you so. You gotta do somethin'."

I tightened inside at the last revelation. I had become attached, as I did too many times, to the stray hound who was past time allotted until euthanasia. This painful dilemma usually was saved by at least one of twenty-three cages being free by nightfall.

147

"Put her outside in a run, please," I said. "We will see what the day brings. I'll go to Banko's and then be in."

"No you won't. They got serious horse trouble up at Joby's place. I said you'd be in touch soon's I could reach you," she countermanded.

"I'll call 'em. Good-bye," I answered.

I called Joby's place and found that the horse had fallen in the swimming pool and they only needed help to get her out as she seemed content to stand in the shallow end. I assured them I could be there soon marveling at the new wave of horse owners dependent on me. They love their pets but have an unexpected lack of horse sense. The happy new owners have no conception of the volume of water a large beast needs and when the supply dwindles, beloved pets wander through inadequate fences directly to pools that are usually surrounded with slippery tile. The horses end up puzzled but patient in azure water reeking strangely of chlorine.

This moment, however, belonged to Joe Banko's "blue roan killer cow," as Joe called her, who badly needed her horns docked. This was confirmed as I finished my trip down the ladder of the side-hill barn and a swishing-swiping horn engaged my jacket over an animal-polished wooden manger.

"Told ya', Doc," Joe's voice cracked from behind the cow. "You sure we can handle this critter?"

I was wary, but I needed a brave helper.

"No sweat, Joe," I said as I lifted her tail, side-stepped an expected kick and injected a wonder drug into her caudal tail vein.

148

In a few moments I could easily duck the laconic lunges of her horns and put in a nose lead. Blocking the nerves to her horns with novocaine was simple then and Joe and I, each with our arms manipulating the oak handles of a big guillotine type dehorner, snapped off her mature, cement like horns with a pop that startled the other barn creatures and specially a bantam rooster in the rafters above. While I was pulling arteries to control bleeding I told Joe that was one fine rooster. The best I had seen for miles around.

"Huh, he's okay, I guess, Doc..but he don't breed no chicks," Joe said with a forlorn look. "I think he's one of them you know...like we're gettin' a lot of around here."

"Oh, you mean the homosexuals that are buying up country homes," I said, trying to ease Joe's parochial mind into conversation.

"Yep, them," he croaked. "I even tried to give him to the Reverend but he said no."

"Why the Reverend?" I asked naively.

"Gawd, don't ya' know, Doc? He's queer too," stated Joe firmly.

"I see," I said, briefly grinning at the floor and made my way to the car.

*****

A sharp-shinned hawk dipped down in front of my windshield as I climbed the tar drive to Joby's house on the hill.

In her talons she carried, under laboring wing beats, the dangling body of a snake to tear up and share with her brood in the locust tree nearby. I pulled my truck up even with a newly laid-up stone wall containing a manicured lawn even with the top on the other side. Across the lawn I saw Joby himself in a lawn chair reading a paper and next to him

the head and shoulders of his mare seeming to arise from the ground itself as the pool was not visible along this line of sight. I approached Joby.

He set the Wall Street Journal down and said, "How about this mess? What the hell's the matter with that horse?"

"I guess she was thirsty and I'm not surprised she fell in considering the footing," I noted. "Who is responsible for feeding and watering?"

"It's the kids' project and they learned all they know from the Carters who are experienced horse people," he said, protecting himself.

I laughed and said, "Yup. They've had horses two whole years now."

"I'm glad I bought this place out of the city," he said not catching my meaning at all, "but for sure, I don't need this shit."

As he spoke he indicated the multiple horse droppings bobbing around in his squeaky-clean pool and an unconcerned horse standing comfortably, though somewhat puzzled, at the shallow end. To the urban oriented, droppings, even of herbivores, are the end-all of pollution though they spend their concentrated lives among man-made chemicals infinitely more lethal.

150

"Many of my friends want to buy places up here," he proclaimed, "because they think it's a good investment, to say nothing of escaping crowds, crimes, and crummy surroundings. They all love animals like I do but they don't know about the nutty things they do and all the bugs that go with them.

"I've noticed a lot of city folks coming," I said, "and many of my clients have been asked to sell their home farms at prices that surpass their tallest dreams. They are hesitant because of close ties to the land in their souls and fear of the government taxation that is wedded to every deal. Most of the offers are twenty times what has been spent on the places over a hundred years and the unrelenting capital gains scare them..as well it should."

"Doc, they seem to resent us city people. Why?" he asked.

I knew shaky ground when I felt it but also knew Joby needed and could handle straight talk. Someone in the new urban arrivals should carry the word.

"Basically they fear you," I said, "because of your daily lack of understanding of how the structure of the country side operates by natural laws and the delicate precious natural balance we live in here. Country people have lived by traditional understanding of those things and stay wary of the paranoia and aggression shown by urban folk who were brought up thinking the only forces out there were economics and efficiency. The clashes will continue in different ways depending on the wisdom of the clashers and general understanding won't be along for years."

"Lordee, Doc. You were ready for that one," he exclaimed.

"I guess I was, Joby, but I didn't know it," I answered. "But let's get the beast out. I'm busy today."

So saying, I put my rope on the mare's halter and handed the end to Joby.

"Take it around that tree trunk...loosely and urge her to the pool edge. When she starts out keep a firm lead so she can use her neck muscles, but DO NOT pull her on to her chin," I instructed.

I grabbed a broom nearby and waited until the horse was moved to the pool corner while I talked to her and stroked her. At the edge I told Joby to give a little slack and then keep it taut when she raised her front end.

"Wot the hell are you gonna do?" he squawked. "Request her to get out?"

"You'll see," I said as I sauntered to the horse's rear and gave her a resounding painless smack with the wet broom. Very quickly she was standing beside an astounded Mr. Joby and shook water all over him.

"Jeez!" was all he said as he shook his head.

Shortly I was on the phone in the cabana telling Boss Lady I was headed her way.

"Well, it's about time," she said. "Mrs. Barker called and said her temperature is only 97 and she's making a nest."

"Mrs. Barker or her little dog?" I quipped.

"Jeesus, Doc. You know, the little dog. It's happening like you said. Today's the day! You better talk to her right now," she bossed.

"I will. No hurry. I'll be there in ten minutes. You get ready for office hours and then surgery, please."

"Jeeesus," she groaned and slammed the phone down.

"How much?" Joby asked as I readied to leave.

"Fifty'l do it," I returned, thinking it was high yet deserved for a half hours know-how plus lecture.

"Boy, you work cheap. That's a bargain. Here, keep it," he said peeling off a clean hundred.

"Thanks a lot," I replied happily. "That's another thing that separates you from the locals. Not only do you always deal in larger amounts than the people here are used to, but the things you advertise in the publications you control seem superfluous and really unnecessary to rural life. They do see quality in most of it but the useful value is really lost to them. For example you don't need all those expensive four wheel drive vehicles and you don't need oil-treated Australian coats from the outback at three hundred a pop. Two thousand dollar burglar alarms can be replaced by twenty dollars worth of dog and you don't need fifteen hundred dollars worth of equipment to go fly fishing."

"Yes, well what the hell! You were ready for that one too, Doc," Joby muttered and turned away - a smile and a frown on the same face.

*****

I drove the few miles to my hospital on the main two lane between gorgeous hillsides and thought seriously of my many dairy clients. Machinery prices and taxes going up, land values going up, labor impossible to find while young family members impelled to urban areas by TV....All this while prices for their product remained the same.

I was able to see this trend long before they did and my answer was to go to Kentucky and learn the practical parts of horse medicine from renowned practitioners. The farmers struggled to make ends meet by trying to handle more cows per man. All their "improvements" were mechanical in nature and cows, being biological, suffered cruelly from overcrowding and confinement. In the end about eighty percent of the farmers went out of business and milk remained in strong supply country wide from huge farms with hundreds of cows, each bearing a number instead of the endearing names the family farms had used. These animals are packed in, fed by computer according to their production, milked by mechanics who curse them, and used as components toward an end product. No more the loved, familiar beasts the country people once knew.

I was building a strong horse practice among the moneyed people that arrived in my verdant parish, and my good fortune was to have real insight into the equine personality. I came to love horses deeply. People could see that and my income held while that of dairymen declined. Their genes, traditional wisdom, spiritual confidence, and strengths still course through the cultural fabric of this wondrous land and hopefully will be a bulwark against the fleeting psychic epidemics that pass for knowledge or "cool" among the increasing numbers of people raised insulated from natural harmony.

I parked my truck at the hospital garage, grabbed two pairs of dirty cover-alls, my heavily used medical bag, and paper work recording farm calls, and tramped across the asphalt to the entrance. During the trip I made sure the garage was open for the phoebes nesting inside, and waved to a milk truck driver I knew as he roared by in flashing stainless steel containing milk for cities to the south. The chipmunks living in the wall under the magnolia were squeaking in alarm as I went by. I walked through the then empty waiting room, the exam room, and the surgery to my office which Boss Lady had made shining and spotless. My desk stood out as a mild jumble with important papers on top. I spied a lab report saying Mr. Beel's mare, "Angel", was pregnant and a card reminding me of a county medical meeting that night at seven.

"That little fuzzy dog keeps laying on his back and usually is licking his side. Did you get the horse out, POOR BABY?" Boss Lady squawked as she approached.

Out of twelve patients in the ward, Boss Lady had picked out the one abnormality I was waiting for to clinch a diagnosis. She often did this and I depended on natural knowledge she didn't know she possessed. In general practice covering many species (ergo many life styles) a doctor does not often have the time needed for proper observation of an intricate case and needs an astute nurse. Her ability to know normal from abnormal is priceless.

155

"Surgery on that pup in about an hour. She's got something stuck. I also have to keep moving to make a county meeting tonight," I said.

"Did you call Mrs. Barker yet?" she stormed.

"Get her on the phone, please," I countered. I'll dump these coveralls then you clean up my medical bag while I catch up on the other phone calls. Office hours in ten minutes."

"Oh, my God. I'll never get out of here," she groaned.

Fortune smiled warmly as hours were simple and rapid with many new puppies for vaccines and physicals. There is always a spate of new pets in the spring and I love the happy pups and proud owners. I dislike the change to frowns, canine and human, that show after painful injections, and lectures on proper care. The puppies' outgoing friendliness change to a suspicious puzzled glance as they go out the door because, as they see it, an understanding human stuck a piece of steel in them when they were really being good.

There were no new cases to admit and Mrs. Barker had reported that her dog had done everything I had said she would about whelping. At the moment she was lying quietly, though panting, in her clothes closet upstairs. I said I would check before I left for the meeting tonight and within an hour I was scrubbed and gloved and deep in the abdomen of the pup with the intestinal obstruction. These were the days before lawyers cranked the profession toward really expensive time consuming lab tests and x-rays before surgery when people trusted my instinct to open an abdomen and save a life. There are a multitude of cases to prove it in my and other practices and our best was good enough for all. New graduates live now in fear of litigation and the costs get higher and higher daily.

My great nurse watched me carefully and was always aware of all the physical things I had taught her in order to watch for signs of trouble with anesthesia or other physiological emergencies. Triumph dawned as I removed the rubber ball blocking the caecum and we finished the delicate bowel surgery, wrapped the pup in a tight belly bandage and Boss Lady whisked her off to a cage she would lace with excess pillows and blankets.

"Now I've got you from that mean man," she said leaving. "You're mine now, Poor Baby, and I'll take care of you."

I knew she would and smiled in relief for the dog and warmth for this deeply blessed animal woman.

The only thing left on my schedule was an appointment twenty miles away to remove some extra teeth from a two year old colt. I might even get a shower before leaving for the meeting with colleagues I was dying to talk to and be with. Hearts, minds, and ears that truly understand without explanation are a welcome and necessary respite from a tense world. The beer doesn't hurt a bit either...and sometimes you even learn something.

It was four-thirty as I headed for my vehicle feeling good about the fuzzy pup I had worried about for the two nights it took for the owner to finally bring it in. I was pulling away from the hospital when a frantic Boss-Lady waved me down and said there was a really upset lady on the phone with an emergency. I thought, of course there is, as time was flying along without me.

157

"My poor baby has been very ill all day since early and I'm worried. I'll bring her right down", an imperious concerned voice proclaimed.

"What are you looking at?" I asked.

"My dog, Doctor. What do you think?" asked the lady.

"I mean the symptoms," I said to this really clear thinker.

"Well, since breakfast she's been drooling and rubbing her cheek on the sofa and now she's very depressed and I'm worried. I'll be there in half and hour."

"Mrs. Koopong", I said, trying to be patient, "I've been in the hospital for two and one half hours. Why didn't you come for office hours? I'm just leaving for an appointment at a horse farm!"

"You are always out for those horses" she said. "What will I do? You haven't failed me before. I had friends in for luncheon so I couldn't come. I supposed you would have time for me at day's end."

I laughed and said, "Too many people think that way about doctors. I'll be at your home in twelve minutes. It's on my way."

"Oh, my!" she panicked. "I hope I'm ready."

"On my way," I exclaimed and hung up.

Her Mercedes was parked at the front door so I stopped short and picked my way through the impatiens, lobelia, and sedum in the border garden and rang the chimes at this gorgeous, well manicured home. The maid, a charming black girl in a tiny frilled apron looked up at my six foot three inch frame topped by a smiling white face above brilliant white coveralls.

"I'm here to look at your little dog."

158

I caught a flicker of humor cross the features of this attractive face as she smiled with alarming beauty and said,

"Yassuh. Y'all come right in."

I knew she had spent since luncheon hour serving spoiled wealthy white people and chided, "What all did you feed that dog?"

"Oh, she got a chicken bone in her teeth but nobody listens to me. I see you're ready for it," nodding toward the sponge forceps in my hand.

Recognizing a kindred soul I whispered, "Please get that pup and bring it here so I don't have to deal with the Misses!"

She giggled and whispered, "Right here in the kitchen, this-way" and disappeared down the right hand hall.

This super girl had the pup on the table as I came into an stocked kitchen, and in a flash I had the lodged bone out of the rc the mouth and was headed out through the foyer as Mrs. Coping's came from upstairs,

"I'll only be a moment, Doctor. Please be seated. Jenny, are you there?"

Blessed Jenny said rapidly,

"Weez okay, Mrs." as I went out the door on my way again.

Great girl, I thought as I leapt into my truck greatly relieved I didn't have to go through traditional murmurings and posturings with that lady who, it seems, has never been in a hurry in her entire life. A week later she stopped at the hospital to pay her bill and told me "Baby Dog" was fine and to gush about the wondrous service.

159

The drive from Mrs. Koopong's to the farm where the colt awaited me was only ten country miles and only took fifteen minutes. When I drove in the long entrance to a beautifully maintained colonial northeast farm I spotted Charlie, Mr. Bux's groom, walking a two year old Thoroughbred colt who watched my car with flared nostrils, erect ears, and a gait that seemed never to touch the ground. The young animal had all the power, beauty, and presence that makes us all love them so. I complimented Charlie on the horse's condition and growth.

"I always knew how to do that. My Daddy said I knew more than he did after he taught me," Charlie said proudly. "He's quick though, Doc! Stay up on the bit when you're near him."

The pulsating combination of curiosity and fear, as he watched my bright, white coveralls coming nearer, had already suggested I stay alert.

"Let me have the lead shank, Charlie," I said. "He needs to know me a little before we get started."

I walked the prancing, skittering colt down the road and on the return trip he walked calmly beside me as he saw Charlie and the familiar barn ahead. From the wild rose hedge beside me a brown thrasher flew in front of the colt and, with that excuse, he reared and pawed. I laughed and gave him slack to complete his front stage act, and he eyed me with approval.

The "wolf" teeth, as horsemen call them, are extra teeth in front of the pre-molars in the space reserved for the bit. When training a young animal to accept a bit the vestigial teeth sometimes give sharp pain from looseness or because the lip gets

160

pressed against them. With mild sedation I lifted them from a shallow bed in the gums with a small tooth elevator.

Charlie said, "Geez, Doc. They came out slick! Like a rich feller gettin' into heaven. You're good with a horse."

Charlie will never know how I value a compliment like that- extemporaneously and from an experienced horseman. I glowed inside as I packed my gear and headed for my cabin in the forest nearby to take a shower.

*****

The meeting was great, as always, and happily held no threat of superfluous continuing education that we all easily got elsewhere. There were, however, many stories of common problems told by wildly different personalities. Friendship and beer made a few hours flash by and as I was leaving I called Mrs. Barker.

"Nothing has happened since I called at ten," she said. "She is still pushing now and then."

Apparently the lady had called my answering service and they had not called me. By now this good lady was worried.

"Mrs. Barker, I'm here at a meeting and had a few beers. If you would prefer to call someone else I don't mind. Though I would have no problem."

"Mr. Barker and I figured you were at a meeting and we would rather have you, beers or not," she said.

With that along with Charlie's compliment I was ten feet tall and could do anything.***********

161

CHAPTER TEN: Friday

My mind focused on Barker's dog as I left the Inn and my car clock read twelve-twenty AM. It was now Friday. I was tired, but needed, and vibrantly alive.

The hills, draped in dancing mist, seemed silent as I dropped to the river valley wherein lay my office. The light at my doorway came into view as I left the shadowed pines, and its halo lighted the sign stating who I was. I was well aware of my identity and pleased with the knowledge. I recalled many agonizing days of hope as a committee at the university deliberated my future. My admission to that great college brought a tidal wave--an epiphany of joy, after years of hope!

The little dog, "Detroit", led the two worried Barkers through the door. In the dog's eyes and body language I saw three things right away; "I know who you are. I'm a little worried about this belly ache. do you suppose you can help these two? They have been screwy all day!"

Mr. Barker lifted Detroit to the table and after clipping her south end and scrubbing her I slipped a latex sheathed finger into her vaginal canal. She turned, bared her teeth and signaled that I had lost my educated mind and had become perverse. I could just feel the tiny puppy rear with tail and both back feet entrapped forward in the pelvic inlet.

"This is a classic breech lock", I told the Barkers and gave the dog a heavy dose of morphine while dodging her flashing teeth.

The next few moments were spent explaining some of the general facts about the surgery and I asked Mrs. Barker if she could help with drugged puppies in spite of the mess of this operation.

"No sweat," the great lady said. I believed her, and was pleased that I would not have to bother Jacqueline, my other nurse. Blond, blue-eyed, and gifted. Unfailing in their abilities, she and her husband worked endless days and played hard as well and I could avoid waking them. I took a look at "Detroit" who was leaving us all to a morphine induced wonderland with a glassy, happy stare and she lolled her tongue from the side of her mouth. I flipped her over, clipped her abdomen--now a startling field of magical mammary mountains----scrubbed her well and set a long line of anesthetic down her mid-line. "Detroit" could care less as she lay singing a quiet drugged aria.

After proper scrubs I made a long incision down her mid-line between sterile drapes and my latex covered hands delivered into view a massive gravid uterus squirming with puppies. I cut into the top surface of the organ and began handing puppies - each with a peeled out placenta - to Mrs. Barker. With my directions, as I reconstructed the chaos, the good lady tore membranes from their little noses and rubbed with towels until the surgery was filled with the delightful squeals of pups and the soothing murmurs of the "parents". The immediate appeal of the tiny creatures had delivered Mr. Barker from his despair at all the blood, mucus, and unwelcome anatomy, to joyous participation helping his wife with tears of relief and happiness in his eyes.

163

All babies were fine and triumph pervaded my clinic. From beneath the drapes, as I put her back together, "Detroit" keened her mournful morphine melody unaware of her wondrous success.

Later I ushered them, a grinning couple, a doped up mother, and a towel-draped box of warm, wiggly puppies, out the door. A glance at the clock showed 2:25 AM and I drove to my cabin for a needed sleep. Alone--no wife, no brown-haired girl, only my setter who welcomed me with unrestrained joy.

*****

After four hours of superior type sleep, my dog and I were en route to a young girl's barn to see a cut and bleeding horse. The route was over a winding dirt road I used very often. The slanted sun sparkled the dew on under brush like a jeweled corridor and dew-laden spider-webs shone like a thousand diamond tiaras. A movement on a slope above me focused my eyes on a young doe in the road ahead with twin fawns at her heels. The trio moved ahead of my slowed car with the twins trying to turn and see what they had come upon that was now following them. Their mother, having seen cars before, stamped an impatient forefoot at the children's delay. At that instant, between she and the fawns and I, there flew from the hardwood forest a huge Barred owl headed to roost from a night of hunting. The big bird banked through a shaft of sunlight through mist, the doe glowered at it, the babies stared in wonder, and I was sure the byways of my life coursed through heaven and

164

not just toward it. Further on the kids waiting for buses shouting and waving, "hi Doc!" convinced me of it.

In the barnyard there stood a bay horse looking embarrassed as its young and worried owner showered the leg with cold water. A pair of blue-jean covered legs on the other side of the animal's neck showed that someone competent soothed and steadied the horse really confused now by the anxious change in routine and the smell of blood.

I spoke to the patient and bent to see a severed artery that was spurting but was easily controlled with finger pressure. A warm strong hand cupped my neck below my ear, then moved slowly to my shoulder muscles under my shirt and gently massaged.

"Not so bad is it, Bub," said a soft voice. I looked up into Crystal's ruddy face and then down her open shirt as she bent over still holding the horse. I gulped and crashed into a whole new world of emotions.

"I guess you mean the leg," I sort of croaked, "no, not bad. Good to see you again."

She was older now and I knew she had planned it this way. Her Dad's farm was nearby and she was a close friend of the horse's owner.

The cut was handled with only a pressure bandage and a promise to return for redressing in a few days. Animals are not really apt to follow orders so I left a woven stretchable bandage to use firmly if activity caused more bleeding.

I turned out of the barnyard as the owner returned the beast to his stall and there, beside the barn door, stood Crystal, her hand in a tight hind pocket her hips cocked. She gave me a knowing smile, and, after a gentle lascivious wave, moved her hand to slowly caress her breast.

I drove back over the countryside waving back to country folk in the freshening sunlight. I wondered at mature me responding in every way dictated by evolution to an irresistible natural country girl. Probably just compatible pheromones, I told myself. I knew that only my constantly busy and thoroughly rich life kept me from a scrambled emotional storm. I roared with happy laughter understood only by me and my sympatico dog in the passenger seat.

*****

I had started to worry about a new client who had called as I left my cabin. She had said that her young Australian shepherd was not quite right, and I had asked her to stay near a phone There was no answer when I called from the barn I had just left. I turned into a small diner as I needed food as well as a telephone. Again there was no answer so I sat at the counter to eat.

Certainly many of my happiest hours have been spent in cafes, diners, or coffee shops. I have always been drawn to them all over America and to their counterparts in other countries. People, happier than they are ever conscious of being, gather for eggs, hashbrowns, fresh pastries, ham, sausage, bacon, or a short

166

stack of wheats. All the time with laughing waitresses, foggy windows, raucous humor, and endless defining of how a government must be run. All this is fueled, in overdose, by the wonder-drug, coffee. I love it all.

I also have noted that all waitresses west of Pennsylvania, if they have a moment, grab a pot and offer refills all down the line while trading saucy remarks and bits of news. This delightful, constructive practice has been lost in the East due to oddball paranoia about cost cutting.

I was talking to a heavy equipment operator next to me when a plate hit the counter in front of me. When I turned to look at my order of "eggs up" nestled between sausage and hashbrowns, in the center of each yolk was a tiny dollop of ketchup. These were obviously "nipples" and I looked up at a buxom girl and stared as her eyebrows waved a lustful message. My friends around the counter roared with laughter and urged my pursuit of the lass into the kitchen. Happiness like that dwells in you forever but my day was full ahead, as the girl knew,

Since another call to the folks with the Australian shepherd went unanswered, I continued up the road to my office. I had asked them when I left to give me time for the horse and then I would call.

They had either not listened, panicked, or impatiently. called my colleague up the mountain. They were part of a new wave of people arriving among us now and I was probably wrong in assuming that they had the faith in me that my regular clients had.

167

While returning north I was faced, in a blink, by a strange looking, but beautifully cornering car. I recognized it as a Saab and its driver, staring with a frown past a coffee mug on the dash seeing only the road, flashed by on his stress filled flight to embrace some cold and nameless computer. These are new animals to me among the tractors and pick-ups of my world. They seem to hurtle onward, watching only the road, not seeing the creatures they crush, astounded and affronted if they hit a deer, and in their increasing "intelligence" are ready to sue any one for the results of their decreasing wisdom.

Finally, back at my clinic, hardworking Boss-lady screeched from the kennel-room that I was to call the Doc up the mountain before I moved. Sure enough, he told me the folks with the gloomy Australian shepherd were there and did I have it on that new medicine for heart worms.

"Yes," I said, and gave the small dosage I used. I knew that it was contraindicated in those type dogs at regular dosages but in the interest of reducing some shocking drug costs, I was experimenting with a number of dogs. It was working--the other dogs were fine but by current standards I was in the wrong. He said he thought the pup would be okay but I decided to quit the experimenting and went on with the day. The shepherd was fine by nightfall and my colleague had a new client.

Boss-lady was cleaning hard as usual and carried on a running duet with a parrot I was boarding for a friend for a few days. I really enjoyed the bird's intelligence and it was pleasant to have around. My assistant was singing, "Shoo-shoo baby," with the Amazon Green apparently answering in kind. The bird I knew was singing "screw you buddy" as its owner had taught it but I never corrected anything as it made no difference and I loved to listen.

I sat at my desk to open mail (bills), return phone calls, and try to line up the morning in some form of efficient geographical order as I must return at 1 PM for office hours and I had a number of farms to visit.

One call was to Mrs Barker of course, who reported that "Detroit" was gloriously happy with her brood, growled fiercely if anything even approached her "place", and apparently had no interest in her sutures lost now among tumescent breasts.

Almost all my time is spent within the confines of this huge county in the northwest corner of my state but I sometimes am called over the state line to New York where I also carry a license. A cattle dealer over there had left a message that a recent dry cow he had was off feed to a point where he was now worried and would I stop to see her this morning.

I called Harry to guess at an arrival time and his wife answered.

"Jeez Doc, that Harry came in a minute ago fuming like a Jersey bull and sayin' that the damn bitch slunk or slank her calf. Here he is now. Nice to talk to you. Find a girl yet?"

Like all the women before her I suppose (bless 'em) the question was rhetorical but served to let me know she was keeping track (along with her circle of friends.)

Harry roared, "Damn cow had a slinker behind her--forget coming--I'm gonna kill her to save her life." A slinker is an aborted calf.

The cow had just stopped milking (dry) and was therefore a loss as she would not calve and start well again. Harry was saying he must sell her for beef in order to cut his loss.

"Will you test her?" I asked, concerned that the herd was not exposed to aborting diseases.

"God no," squawked Harry, "ya think I'm a rich Vet er sumtin?"

"Well Harry be sure and clean up and keep her away from the herd. Those discharges could be dangerous." I was conscious of the fine fiscal line the current dairymen must tread, so didn't push the issue.

"Thanks Doc. Watch for them rich babes." He hung up fast and I was sure half the world shepherded my social condition. The "rich babes" and others circled like hunting hawks as I hid in the cover of a busy practice. My mind and body thought often of the brown-haired girl and Crystal's animal aura was invasive.

Boss Lady was happily cleaning and singing to the numerous patients in the clinic so I went swiftly to my truck and left. I had two hours to get back for office hours and probably could manage to get to see one more horse at a farm twenty miles away, remove a small eyelid tumor, and return. Five minutes out my radio screeched.

"Come back here! Mr. Bilson needs you for a calving cow right now! There's some girl here you said could go with you today and she just arrived. You left and she might cry!"

I knew the girl, had forgotten she was coming, and was not worried about her crying. Dee was one third of my age, gifted with correct responses in the animal world, and capable of dealing out adequate vengeance for being forgotten in many more subtle and savage ways than tears. I really loved her company, realized she would love to see bovine obstetrics and knew she would be helpful.

"Ask Dee to be out front in 3 minutes." I replied by radio. "Please call to cancel the eye surgery, and tell Mr. Bilson I'll be right there."

"Okay, but don't be late for office hours." The answer came. "We have a lot of work here and I don't have cage room for that Jezebel hound you love!" All of which I really needed.

I swooped through the hospital drive and Dee leapt in a flash of tawny legs, farm-girl muscular arms, and brown but feline eyes.

"Took ya long enuff," she said with an evil smile.

I always really watched this girl and recognized her bid for an emotional bath about my forgetting she was coming. "Gosh I wish you were ten years older".

"If I were I wouldn't be here with an old fart like you," she snapped back.

We smiled at each others smile and knew love was there forever sealed at an age-dictated distance. The trip to the farm took ten minutes--for eight of which Dee gripped my right forearm with two strong hands.

No one was in the barn and I found the heifer in a box stall deeply bedded with straw. She was troubled and my examination, while Dee calmed her, showed me a problem only solved by surgery.

I said, "Dee, I'll need help with a c-section. A fast one as we have to make the office in 80 minutes."

"No problem, just talk," replied Dee.

"Go to the house and get the owner. Call the hospital to tell them what's up while I clip the cow's flank and start some anesthesia."

Dee left without a word and, as I worked I prayed the world would forever treat this girl as the precious jewel she was.

I had the animal lying on her side and was scrubbing her when Dee returned and said, "Boss lady said that it was okay and that you should do it right." Mr. Bilson said to cut away and he has other things to do. What should I do now?"

"Please kneel on the other side of the mother and listen to me."

The animal slept fine as I cut through the belly skin and muscles, isolated the uterus, and removed the monster calf within.

Dee cried softly, "The little thing is inside out! Its heart is right there and its beating and look! there's guts all over!"

I told her I would explain later and removed the fetus. The uterus was retracting as I sutured it and Dee, seeing my problem reached in and grabbed the organ and lifted thereby aligning the

172

incision edges so suturing became easy and fast. The remainder of the procedure was routine and we left the animal resting comfortably. The fetus had died and I dragged it out of the barn while Dee washed blood off the cow and the instruments.

One hour after we left we were returning to the clinic.

"Thank you." I said to Dee. "You were perfect back there."

Dee said definitely and quietly, "Yup."

*****

My parking area held three cars waiting for office calls and in front of the door was parked a Bronco that seemed familiar. We entered a side door and I headed for cleaner over-clothes while Dee gathered up instruments and cover-alls to start cleaning them. Most in the waiting room seemed content; however, a man stood, back to the receptionist's window, staring out the front window. Veterinarians spend a lifetime watching body language and I knew this man was in trouble so I went to him ready for anything.

"Can I help, sir?" I asked.

He stared in answer and then walked out to his car. I could tell he was shocked and followed. He opened the vehicle door and stood back, a look of misery on a now tearful face. I stepped past and looked into an apparently empty car until I spied a taut leash wound around the seat head rest. Behind the seat hung the body of the most beautiful Boxer any where, hanging by a choke chain at his neck. I released him fast but felt death in my arms.

"Its over an hour, Doc, can you handle the body? I only left the car for twenty minutes. I don't know what to do" He said in an empty voice.

I said I would handle everything and, to give him something firm, I asked him to be sure and call in a while--that I needed him to. He nodded and left me with the beautiful dog and my own tears. I carried the body back of the hospital to the freezer used for the deceased and went to face office calls.

With the exception of one striking looking cat the office work was routine. The cat had been "sort of choking" for a week. The owner spoke up. "My cat is special, Doctor. She won't let you near her to examine her. She's a Peruvian Bomber cat that I paid six hundred dollars for in New York. They said she would be like that."

I knew the lady had raised the "Bomber" to be rotten and that she had really been taken in "New York". I also knew that made no difference and asked boss Lady and Dee to get the X-ray ready. The cat's owner put the animal in the waiting room cage for me and reluctantly went home promising to call me in two hours. With boss lady's expert help I gave the snarling and, I knew frightened cat a fast sedating injection. From that point we entered the animal ward and gave injections to two tom cats who were in for castration.

"Please prep the cats for surgery," I said. "Dee and I will radiograph the cat's throat. I think you get enough x-rays in a week and even being careful you should avoid it when you can."

"Well okay, but I feel fine, "she replied.

174

Not wanting to enter a technical discussion I just walked away after nodding wisely.

Dee and I x-rayed the now quiet cat. While the plate developed I explained the abnormal calf to Dee. It was a recognized deviation that occurs in the first days after conception. The very beginnings of the spinal cord are abnormal and do not allow the belly to close over developing organs. Usually the calf can be delivered but this one was presented in such a way that it could not be turned and extracted.

"What'ya call it? asked an interested Dee.

"Shistosomas reflexus", I said, "and you only see two or three in your career"

"What does that mean?", she asked, interested.

"In Latin it means you don't know your butt from a hole in the barn," I replied with the sagest of squints.

"I thought so. Want me to develop the x-ray?" she asked with the devil in her eyes.

"Yup".

At that moment Boss-Lady bellowed, "Those two ball bearing mouse traps are ready to do. Want em?" she said appearing around the corner with an anesthetized cat draped over each arm. "Why do people get cats castrated any way, Doc?", she asked.

"To keep them home, to stop urine odors and fighting, and they think it controls cat population", I answered.

"Oh. The poor things", she said.

I put on gloves and quickly removed the testicles and boss lady carried them back to the ward mumbling about "crazy mean people". She didn't realize how much easier the cat's lives would be.

Dee returned with the cat's picture and I pointed out the narrow line indicating a sewing needle in the base of it's tongue.

"There most likely is a thread going down the throat to the stomach causing the vomiting. I hope it goes no further or we have a bigger problem", I told her.

"How did you know?" Dee asked cutting to the heart as usual.

"Books, I've seen it before, it's not uncommon and I could see she wasn't a sick cat," I told her.

Dee and I anesthetized the sedated cat, backed the needle out, and carefully pulled the thread from the stomach.

At that moment there was a horn outside.

"That's my boyfriend, "Dee said. "I'd really rather stay but-you know."

"I'm gonna hang myself, Dee" I muttered hanging my head.

Dee snapped, "Okay, but wait 'til I graduate from Vet School will ya? Somebody has to do things right around here!"

"Deal," I said. She hugged me fiercely and flew out the door. Before it closed I stopped her and said, "Tell your friend that real men don't beep horns, they come in to get a lady and when they do, the hat comes off!"

She grinned and assured me she would straighten him out or get rid of him!

My watch said four-thirty, which was the time I was due at a farm to examine a lame horse. The little mare was due to be shown on Sunday and had come in lame the night before. She trotted with a slight nod to her head and would be eliminated from classes at the show that she had been entered in and paid for months before. Her training represented years of patient skillful work with these types of shows as her target.

The diagnosis of lameness in horses, if not obvious, is accomplished by using nerve blocks from the bottom up and seeing in between each one if you are able to end the lameness with the block. Then you often must x-ray, having found the general area. In this case, when I lifted the lower leg to use the blocking injection, I felt the horse, with my body against her, slightly wince from firm hand pressure. I didn't need the block and then found pain on compressing a cartilage just at the hoofline.

This horse I had known for years. At the time I set the hoof down she turned and almost nodded just as Elisa, the owner, was doing the same. The Horse, an Arabian cross, watched with huge intelligent, brown eyes as we talked.

"Elisa, in order to make the show we have one option. I want to inject a powerful anti-inflammatory behind that cartilage."

She replied quickly, "Anything you say Doc. Lets get at it".

Elisa I had known for over twenty years. Nearing forty she carried herself with confidence, was muscular where other women jiggled, and had brown hair bordering on red pulled back into a firm attractive braid. Her boots were worn from years of riding but well cared for and likewise soft riding britches well fitted over her haunches. This last I had checked on faithfully for those 20 years.

"Get your twitch please, Elisa", I said. "Don't want this friend of yours to move during injection. It's near too many things that are important."

"Gotcha," she said, and reached to the barn wall to grasp a wooden handle with a loop of chain attached to one end. She placed the loop over her horse's upper lip and wound it up only firm enough to hold it on. The lovely animal knew the tool and knew that in Elisa's hands would be used only lightly to control and communicate. I know of no crueler tool in the hands of the many out there that simply have no idea how it is supposed to be used. Especially on the horse who has never seen one before.

This real horsewoman tightened only slightly at my signal and gently vibrated the handle as I completed the cortisone injection with ease.

"Cold showers as often as possible today and tomorrow please, El", I instructed, "and the best of luck on Sunday".

"Thanks, Doc," she said, and in her pragmatic and striking green eyes I saw a fleeting moment of gratitude and deep warmth. With a lady like this, and I've known many, that's all you're gonna get other than bills paid on time. I knew that the day was coming that I would miss these ladies and their incomparable and beloved equine partners very, very deeply. Oh yes, I will also be sad not to meet again their farm dogs and cats and their resident Muscovy ducks and Bantam chickens.

On the trip back to the hospital I called on my radio to see if anyone was there. Frequently everyone goes home and I am left with a few hours work without the staff's able assistance.

This time, however, Boss lady answered with a roar, "What d'ya want? I want to get outta here!"

I said, "Okay, is there anything you need and has any more happened?"

"There's a couple of phone calls you gotta return and I tied your lover dog, Jezebel, to the column down in the ward. Remember there are no cages free. Your problem- you handle it. She sure is a lover. I suppose you will have to kill her." she answered .

The rest of the way back I thought of so many stray dogs I had had to put down. For most there was no other way. They were untrained and homeless and the majority of people could not handle them. They were strays, in the most part because their owners had no knowledge of training. Now they hardly missed them and, within a year they will get another puppy, only to repeat the process.

Later on, in a deserted hospital while rubbing Jezebel's ears, I struck upon a thought that smacked of genius. The dog and I had a love affair going but Mr. Nichols, the seriously saddened owner of the gruesomely deceased boxer, badly needed this loving dog in his now empty widowed life. In a moment I had him on the phone:

"Oh, hello, Doctor," a defeated voice said quietly.

"I need some help, Mr. Nichols. I often don't have cage room for a stray hound here at the hospital. I really like her but I'm under pressure to put her to sleep and I can't. Could you please watch over her for a few days at your house?" I asked feeling like a sly horse trader.

"Oh yes, Doc," a brighter, stronger voice said. "You helped me a lot. It's the least I can do. I'll be right over."

In about an hour Mr. Nichols was walking out the door with a flirting Jezebel beside him. I knew Jezebel would finish the job but just before jumping in the Bronco she turned and our eyes met for a fleeting contact that will haunt me forever.

The plan succeeded with joy all around and my dog thrilled that she would no longer have to put up with the scent on my clothes of the luscious "Jezebel". I would never have put her to sleep!

I remember that dog to this day as representing all those I had to kill because they had no one. There were tears under pressure behind my eyes and other veterinarians feel this way too, though they may never speak of it.

Evening was upon me as I finished paying bills and I was feeling my short rest time of the previous night. I had started out the door thinking warm thoughts of my beloved cabin and of the sleep I would get in the familiar forest. After a screech of brakes a pickup careened into the drive and a client jumped out. The smell of beer preceded him but I recognized him as a friend and fellow ball player. This was Barlow, a truck driver and small farm owner, whom I enjoyed immensely and who had helped me often

180

with practical things in the past. He claimed, with gusto, that doctors had no practical knowledge. As a cow obstetrician and sometime orthopedic surgeon, I disagreed, but allowed his triumph for I liked him and often needed his talent.

"Damn dog keeps tryin to puke," he said, acting as if he didn't care that much. "I am ready to put a bullet in her."

By now I knew people well and his bravado covered a deep worry. I also was alerted by what he had said and asked him to get the big shepherd as soon as he could

"Great," he said, having transferred his responsibility to me. "She's right in the truck, Doc. I'll git her. Damn bitch!"

In a man like this, this is an expression of love.

When the big dog descended from the truck my fear that she was bloated was confirmed. After eating and with some play-like exercise, the stomach on deep-chested dogs can turn on its long axis thereby closing the exit and entrance. Gas soon accumulates and the animal is in danger of dying badly due to bacterial shock.

With the able and scared help of Barlow, I sedated the lovely dog and with good fortune, passed a stomach tube. Some times you can't and you must go to surgery. In this case the gas was released in a torrent relieving my concern and further greening Barlow's complexion!

I removed the tube and said, "Barlow, pick up your dog by the front half and walk around the room jiggling her gently. This ploy tends to help the stomach return to normal position."

Barlow looked at me as if I was freaky but did the job with confidence, strength, and wonder.

"Your dog will be fine now, Bub," I said.

Barlow looked at me with wide open shiny eyes and left the room. After giving him a few moments, I went in and remarked, "real men DO cry, Barlow old buddy. Now you know for sure."

He carried his logy dog to the pickup seat and with a mumbled, "Thanks a bunch, Doc," drove off.

A week later he stopped in, plunked a six-pack on my desk, and paid his hefty bill as the shepherd wagged her tail beside him. For him the brew was the ultimate gift. For me the whole episode joined many others that create in my soul the confidence and joy that filled my life.

Later, finally at my cabin, I popped a big potato in the micro wave and when I finished a steaming shower, devoured it and vaulted into a chest-high bed built into the wall with solid oak and barn beams for legs. I built it that way to be at window level and closer to my much loved forest and its creatures.

It was nine-forty-five and as soon as I fell asleep the phone rang twice in succession. One call was about a puppy with diarrhea, and later as I dropped off, a call about a horse off his feed for a few days. Both I could put off till tomorrow. I cursed the instrument but

if I didn't have a phone I couldn't spend the time there that I did. I generally covered it twenty-four hours a day except for Tuesday night to Wednesday night. People have no idea of a doctor's schedule and call when they worry. This will never change and I would rather talk then than get a case too late to help. Putting them off requires careful questioning and good judgment. All of that you get from experience. It also needs client confidence in you and, for the most part, I had that.

Sleep came easily and I looked forward to Saturday, and beyond that, Tuesday night and Wednesday that were critical to keep me focused on my wondrous life. I dreamed of Crystal!

****

CHAPTER ELEVEN: Saturday

There was a deep rumbling growl from my dog nearby and my eyes snapped open to see the first lights of dawn over the huge pines outside. I put down my inclination to move and give away my location because that growl means only that things are not normal. Abnormal can vary here from a coon or skunk on the porch to a deer in the grove or a car parking nearby. I listened for a few moments and then eased my hand over to grasp an automatic that has been somewhere close since the days of war. The growl went on with increasing volume so I levered a round into the breech, and rested my thumb ahead of the hammer as my habit has been. I heard the soft sound of the sliding door as it slid on its vinyl track. My great dog snarled as a figure moved in the dark and I snapped on a light positioned for just this reason with a switch near my hand. In the light's beam I looked over my sights at a seriously squinting Crystal.

"That's what I like about you," she said calmly. "You stay alert. Never saw you miss a thing."

"What's wrong, Crystal?" I asked. I knew it was the stupidest question of my life.

"Are you kiddin', Bub,? You and I knew this was comin' since I was a little kid. I adore you, so move over while I get these clothes off," she said with her customary on-target country wisdom.

With that she kicked off her shoes, unsnapped her jeans and allowed them to fall while she peeled her shirt over her head, then stood quietly using one foot and then the other to pull off the opposite jean leg and sock. The movement necessary for this left me breathless watching her almost perfect body now clad only in a bra that not quite did its job to contain high firmly rounded breasts and panties clinging to the most gorgeously curved muscular hips I have seen anywhere.

I thought I should say it so I did.

"Are you sure about this Crystal? You are twenty years my junior!"

"Yup. Would you unsnap my bra while I think about it?" she said moving to the high bed and turning her back.

I could see then that this was all pre-planned so to gain some initiative I said, "Nope, pants first," and peeled off the seriously challenged bikini, put one arm around her chest and the other firmly between her legs from behind and lifted that laughing warm woman to a position on top of me.

My memory cannot do justice to the ensuing two hours, but I recall that I later slept cradled in Crystal's strong arms my face against her breast. This natural nurturing country girl-woman let nothing prevent her from holding me in that manner as she ran over all the ways I had helped her animals and fed her fantasies since she was a child. Her family was strongly made and her mature mind knew that this was a one-time thing. Now and then we wave from afar or simply stand and warmly-quietly stare at one another across varying scenes. I will not forget the power of her arms and thighs, nor the scent of her young body, nor the sounds from her lips as they gripped my ears that dawn. Very, very close, yet far apart.

Crystal and I said good-bye in a steaming shower stall. I stood behind her and she had reached back to grasp my buttocks and press me against hers. The hot water struck the back of my neck and thence over her hair. Talk was not needed and the moment remains within.

*****

For veterinarians, Saturdays seem to be the busiest of days. People, busy with work during the week bring their pets for routine care. Horses also need medical care and owners figure that Saturday is best since they are home. Husbands are more often available to help with intractable pets or children. Saturday office hours start at ten AM and often run to one or two PM.

On the way to my office I stopped to see the horse that had been not eating. Roger's horse stood at about seventeen hands, meaning that this animal was looking DOWN at me. In this instance that was lucky as it put me in a perfect position to be hit by the memorable odor of dead flesh emanating from his mouth. I took his tongue in my hand to the side and with it forced his jaw open to spot a length of green tree branch forced between the rows of teeth and imbedded in the hard palate. Horses put up with this handling of the tongue very well if done with firm gentleness and no fear. With a little instruction, Roger controlled the animal as I took a brief moment with pliers and removed the stick. I gave the patient animal a dose of Penicillin and a tetanus booster and continued on to the office.

*****

At my office there was a pickup and horse trailer blocking most of the parking space and I saw that it belonged to a big man named Frank, a capable horseman who owned the best driving horses around. While I was parking he approached and loudly announced his mission

"I figured you'd be here this mornin' checkin' the damn pussy cats fer the city people. All I need is a blood test fer Coggins. Gotta make a show next week 'n they won't let me in without it. Kin we git at it? Then I'll get on my way," he sort of shouted.

"Sure," I said, as I reached for a syringe and blood vial from my car. "Back him out."

The Coggins test, named after the Veterinarian that perfected it, was to find carriers of an infectious anemia of horses. The animals are tested to eliminate carriers of the disease from large gatherings of horses.

Folks that use driving horses seem to handle them differently from other horsemen in that there is a great deal of loud shouting involved. I used to think they were all frightened of their big beasts until my brown-haired girl gently reminded me

187

that these people handle horses from a carriage and not with gentle movement of their hands and legs from the animal's back!

"Stop hollering, Frank," I said. When he did the horse relaxed and I was able to get a sample from his garden-hose sized jugular. I backed away and the lovely animal, with a curious glance at me from beneath a heavy black forelock, jumped nimbly back into his familiar trailer .

"Thanks Doc. I guess they'll send it to me. Send a bill," Frank said and in a moment he was on the road as promised.

It was about ten AM now and the parking area held three cars all of the very expensive type that week-end homeowners seemed to prefer. Two were larger four wheel drive types driven by small ladies and filled with packages, children, and a pet carrier or happy dog. I had my doubts that they would ever use the four-wheel capabilities but things like that never seem to slow the psychic epidemics that humans undergo concerning possessions.

I went around back and came in through the ward and by the outside runs that held some of the quieter patients. They all seemed to recognize me and wagged and wiggled their varied welcomes. I really loved these moments that were daily occurrences. Not only were they pleasant, but they gave me an accurate assessment of how the patients were doing. There was a tug at my chest, though, as I noted the absence of the warm "Jezebel".

I buttoned on an immaculate white frock over barn smelling clothes, thereby making the psychic change from the pragmatic large animal people to the generally more whimsical small animal practice.

The first case was the little puppy whose owners had called about in the evening before Crystal time and seemed a thousand hours ago. The little creature had had a serious diarrhea then but was surely fine now. The mother said that she had not fed it anything as I had suggested but the kids piped right up.

"I gave him three fig newtons," said one, and the other immediately hollered, "I gave him the cookies. You gave him the Baby Ruth."

"Did not".

"Did too," etc., etc., as the picture cleared up.

"Puppies are like vacuum cleaners," I told the mother. "They eat almost anything in an experimental way. I sometimes wonder how they live through some episodes. I have to cut something out quite often."

"Ye gods," Mom said. "You'd think they'd know better."

"Not me," I said

At that point my alert and sharp blond nurse came up and stated that the pup also had round worms. She had made a slide from the fecal material on the thermometer I had used on the puppy and, as she often did, added another wise dimension from under her microscope. I had started out to train her when she first came to work but now her able mind moved ahead as she trained herself simply by watching me.

189

I gave the pup a needed vaccine, dispensed the correct worm medicine and, with instructions, the family left a bit wiser, I hoped.

As the family was taken out by my nurse I looked across the office back of the exam room having felt the gaze of the brown-haired girl as she stood holding a phone she had just answered. The look I had grown willingly used to and it said to do nothing except to take this call. She was there to do bookwork but grabbed the phone as needed. Flickering through my busy mind in those days was the dancing thought that I loved her. She had been somewhere near for ten busy years.

I took the call.

"Doc, please come now!" cried a panicked voice. "My daughter's horse broke through the barn floor and is hanging there. We need you quickly."

"Where is your daughter?" I asked.

"She's there trying to keep him calm," he answered, quieter now.

They were only a few miles away and I knew the girl and horse to be real partners with a tendency to be calm.

"Good," I said thankfully. "I'll be right there and you get a lot of hay bales to the lower level."

"Right," he said and was gone.

I went immediately to the waiting room and told the two waiting clients what the problem was and that I had to leave. They could wait for my radio call or re-schedule for tomorrow, Sunday morning. One swore but the other gasped hoping that the horse would be okay. The compassionate and the self-centered. They both chose to wait.

The barn was only four miles down towards town and as I drove in toward the barn I could see half a horse apparently imbedded in the hayloft floor. So that I didn't panic the quiet horse and owner I drove around to the lower level. There were three men standing there gazing upwards at the dangling lower half of the same horse. They had plenty of hay bales ready and I asked them to pile the bales, four wide, up to about the level of the hind feet.

I said, "As soon as you can, add bales as he goes up."

Great countrymen that they were they simply nodded, understanding the plan as if I had been there before--which I HADN'T. A Marine Sergeant had told me that if I didn't know exactly what to do--wing it but think! I had a nature that did that anyway.

I went upstairs to the barn floor and as the girl calmed the horse, I clipped a strong rope to his halter and then put my own cotton rope around his belly with a slip knot and with same line took a half hitch around behind his elbows. This line I took around a column ahead of the horse and handled it myself.

I told the resolute girl to handle the halter rope around the same column and to give the horse purchase to use his considerable neck muscles but, if he panicked, give him his head. Female, she knew what I meant. Most men would try to do the whole job with their muscles and would fail.

I asked one of the men downstairs to give the horse a painless but scary whack with a barn broom and then add bales as fast as the horse needed them.

Lady Luck smiled brightly that Saturday and amid cheers the horse soon stood on the upper floor and with dignity accurately defecated through to the groaning men on the floor below. As they laughingly rehashed the great event, I radioed the hospital that I would be there in 15 minutes. The grateful girl and her dad waved as I left and at weeks end he sent payment for twice my bill.

Back at the hospital I went through the change again from coveralls to pristine white frock. I asked the guy who swore at the delay to come in and he entered with a small cat carrier.

"Cat's got a sore neck. My wife can't seem to get anywhere with it and she's tried everything on that damn sore, cat won't eat a thing, think we ought to get another one?" he asked getting it all in one sentence.

The sore went all around the neck --a dead giveaway for those who have seen it before. I cleaned serum and pus from one spot and with a little search, found and cut the offending rubber band placed and forgotten by some youngster. The client swore he would "kill that kid," but I persuaded him to just show the wound to the child and especially let him smell it and the child would never forget or repeat it.

As I accompanied the happy client out of the waiting room I nodded to a Levi clad, tanned and strong young man in the corner. I saw at his feet a mature Australian Heeler dog who politely wiggled a greeting and then flopped down looking unhappy--totally out of character for this great breed. The man was Tony Lake, a good friend and client who worked for the phone company but kept an immaculate farm with beef cattle and horses. The dog was a talented herder of anything.

"Tony," I asked, "what's wrong with Jake?"

"Don't mean to be smart, Doc, but that's why I'm here." Tony said. "He won't eat and don't breath right. Not like him and I'm worried."

Having already noticed the belly breathing and admiring Tony for seeing it too I said, "C'mon in."

On the table then I found some really strange sounds in Jake's chest and a really tucked up and empty abdomen.

"When did he get kicked Tony?" I asked.

"Gawd, Doc. You're sumthin. I got a new filly the other day. Fast with her feet, and Jake found that out right quick. He rolled away from that kick though and I figured he was okay but hasn't eaten since. He won't die will he?" Tony asked really worried.

"Not if I'm right and we get after it. I need a special x-ray now and then I'll tell you," I said and noted that my super nurse and my brown-haired lady were already setting up the machine. They had both known what I was thinking and took immediate advantage of a break in the flow of clients. Bless alert people, I thought, they seem to become more rare each day.

"Tony, if you could stay and help then I won't have to give Jake any sedative to snap a picture," I said, and Tony agreed, happy to help.

I gave Jake a small amount of fluid that would show up in an x-ray and, with Tony calming him, I finished the exposure and we soon had proof that the kick to the little dog's belly had caused some intestine to break through the diaphragm and lodged in the crowded lung cavity.

Tony looked at the picture as I explained it and turned his now very pale face towards me and whispered, "Can you fix him Doc? Jake and I are awfully close since Sabrena left me. I don't know what I'd do without his company now."

Sabrena, a country girl, but lacking Crystal's wisdom and susceptible to television's charm, had left for the city a year ago. Tony was lucky but didn't know it yet.

"It's touchy work Tony," I said, "but I've done it before and I think we will win it."

The man's eyes widened and became shiny. Hoarsely he whispered, "Oh please,Doc," He turned and left after touching Jake who was beginning to feel the strong pre-anesthetic drug I had given a moment before.

I stood again where men of medicine so often do. Nothing was more important to me than to succeed here. Not love, not money, not any god I have proof of. Even people closest to you often forget that this can be a daily condition. It seemed to me the brown-haired girl felt the most as she touched my arm and said nothing.

With only one office call left I asked my nurse to start the now sedated Jake under anesthesia using only a mask for the volatile gas combination that I used for long term surgery. This woman was very adept in watching the critical parameters I had taught her for monitoring depth of anesthesia and this was the safest route. Later I would need to pass a tube into Jake's trachea in order to use positive lung pressure.

Meanwhile the office call was waiting in the exam room. On the table was a gorgeous Chow puppy held proudly by a thirty-something well dressed man that I knew to be a currently popular producer of plays in New York. I remarked,

"That is one good looking dog. What's wrong?"

The gentleman said, "He's very, very valuable. He has had all his vaccines and early tests by the best in the city, but this morning he was limping on his rear leg. I'm really distraught about it!"

The puppy looked at me and his expression said that he agreed and what was I going to do about it?

I asked the owner to walk the puppy across the floor and confirmed the limp and, back again on the table, felt the limb and its joints in great detail according to training and long experience. I leaned on the table and was explaining to the tense owner that it was a strain of soft tissue and would be okay in a day or two and that I wouldn't use pain killers as animals tend to use an injured part too much when you do.

At that the pup turned and took my forearm in his teeth. Knowing full well that I shouldn't move I waited for the shocked owner to convince the dog to let go.

"Please take your valuable dog home," I said, "and don't come back until he has some manners. He had no reason to do that!"

They left without a word and never were to be seen again. The reaction I had was not my nature and though the breed is renowned for that I guess I was worried about Jake and Tony and was not wary. That graceful owner called later to apologize.

Meanwhile, since Jake was sleeping well with the somewhat labored breathing as I would expect with a chest half full of intestines, I put in a tracheal tube and showed my super nurse how she could help him breath by using the re-breathing bag attached.

"Remember that," I said firmly. It will be really critical when I open the abdomen and expose the lung cavity to atmospheric pressure. Jake will surely need us both then."

The dog's abdomen had been shaved and beautifully prepped for aseptic work while I treated my slightly torn arm. After donning sterile gloves I made an incision from his sternum to his umbilicus. I could then see the tear in the diaphragm and enlarging it slightly I was able to retract the offending small intestine from the chest. There was immediately some difficult breathing which, by leaning back and letting my nurse see how she was affecting the rise and fall of the pink lung, she easily corrected.

I said, "When I am closing that tear with sutures keep breathing for him lightly. When I am about to take the last stitch you must fill the lung fully and hold it there until I have made an air tight closure then, when the lung is allowed to retract in exhaling, it will leave a critical negative pressure in the chest but outside the lung."

In her memorable way the head snapped down and up as she whispered tensely, "Right. So he can fill the lung again."

I simply said, 'Right', but could have shouted to the mountains in gratitude for kindred souls. Now women like this have degrees and happily grace my profession with talent, beauty, and are finally armed with efficient birth control thereby practicing medicine instead of motherhood.

I finished the procedure as we had planned and when we both returned Jake to a clean cage with warm blankets I was pleased to see his eyes blink and a wiggle from his tail as I spoke his name.

Meanwhile two more clients were waiting to see me. They had arrived unnoticed either by me or super-nurse, but had been gracefully greeted by the quiet brown-haired girl.

The first to enter was a large and powerful man I knew to be head of a financial company based close to the city. He practically roared announcing his presence.

"Gawd! I thought if I came late I wouldn't have to wait so long. What were you and that neat blondie doing back there anyway?"

"Come in, Jim," I said, not rising to the bait. "What can I do for you?" I knew that false reputations were created in his circle by men like him and similar women seeking recognition.

197

"Dawg's driving me nuts at night. Scratchin', scratchin', scratchin'. Must be the mange or something he got up here in the wild."

Mostly that is the contemporary opinion of the urban wave of people and more often the itching is due to arcane skin sensitivities or to animals genetically designed for colder climates.

"Nice looking dog, Jim. What does he do all day up here?"

"He's in the woods just about all day. God knows what he's up to. But he sure likes it," he said sort of puzzled.

"He's only doing what his genes tell him to do, Jim."

"I suppose so, but last month he killed a fox and dragged it home. I don't go for that too much."

An immediate clue. No dog catches a normal fox and the most common weakening disease in foxes is long standing mange. With a scalpel blade I scraped a suspicious area on the front leg, put the debris on a slide and easily, for a change, found live sarcoptic mites.

"I knew it was mange! I suppose I'll have to get rid of him now. Damn dog!" Jim said, exposing his warm sensitive nature.

"No Jim. That was years ago. I give him an injection and he gets dipped today and then twice more at weekly intervals. Then he's okay."

"Well, what about us? We don't want the damn bug, "he said, scowling.

"You'll be better off now than you have been for the last month and the disease won't stay with you anyway. We have our own mites," I explained.

"Let's get at it, Doc," he said.

"Right. Pick him up between 5 and 6 this evening please."

"See ya' then," Jim said and left.

As I closed the outside door a young girl went in from the waiting room carrying a bundle and talking a mile a minute.

"This is Flossie, my rabbit. She has a sore neck. I'll hold her for you cause she's scared and I know about rabbits," said a definite ten year old girl as she came through the door with a cat carrier in her arms.

"This is Jenny," a patient attractive heavy-weight Mom said, "She does know about rabbits, and that was a long wait. I was told you didn't schedule surgery on Saturdays."

"True," I said. "That was not scheduled. Sorry you had to wait. We all deal with Murphy's Laws in one way or another. I'm sure you do when you have children around. Would you like me to take Flossie from the carrier?"

"No no no. I'll do that," Jenny said somewhat stridently. "Men always grab the skin on the back of a rabbit's neck and rabbits fight so hard they can break their 'verterbers'."

The girl was right and she gently placed Flossie, who I soon noticed was "Fred", on the exam table. I said nothing about the gender and Jenny pointed out an oozing sore on "its" neck. When I wiped away the serum and pus I could see some vague movement at the draining opening and knew what I had. Working

199

fast with Jenny somewhat aghast I snipped the edge of the opening and reached in the cavity with small forceps and pulled out a large, wriggling, grub-like fly larva and placed it on the table for all to see.

Jenny screamed and Mom grasped the table edge.

"What in the hell is that damn creature?" Mom said with proper though somewhat cross-eyed aplomb.

"That is the larva of a fly called Cuterebra," I told them. "It is common here in kittens also. The adult fly places an egg on their skin and the larva penetrates to spend the first of its life under the host's outer layer. Not harmful but you will be a long time healing the sore because of the old scar tissue."

"Do they bother people? Is it possible that they would bother us?"

I told her that in some parts of the world that was true but not here. She mumbled something about the crazy animal world.

"I'll take the mall any day," she said and left.

I could not have disagreed more thoroughly!

The phone had been ringing steadily for the previous three hours and I had to check on what was happening and also knew I had better eat or drop. Typical Saturday - minimal breakfast and no lunch and already it was three PM. But Crystal at dawn! In a flicker my mind registered that life was brilliantly filled but a love was missing.

I had returned many phone calls and the day had boiled down to endless paper work concerning paying suppliers' bills and sending out specimens to laboratories and reports to clients. I had found an apple and a wandering package of crackers to hold a complaining stomach at bay for a while. The brown haired girl was last to leave and stopped to talk a moment.

"You really should talk to someone besides young women and worried clients you know. I have children, dogs, and horses to care for first but could bring some vegetables to cook at your cabin if you could pick up a piece of meat to cook on that outside fire place we built but never see 'til after dark--if then," she wisely suggested.

My mind, on over-load, quickly saw the sense in that and rapidly said, "Good. See ya." That lady had, in the past, helped me gather stones and build the fireplace chimney in the main cabin and I recalled the quiet of the times we had together. She was also conscious of the miles I had to go and knew about when I would get there. I also I knew that, if I was delayed, there would be no comment.

I noticed from that point in a different but parallel part of my mind that there was a feeling of some anticipation and of anxiety ceased. I also, in that one second, realized that that feeling was probably significant.

For now, however, there was another injured horse and also a Llama to be examined for pregnancy and general soundness in order to complete a pricey sale. I figured the miles and weekend traffic would cost me about three hours.

There is an economy that exists far above the normal animal owners'. It is a dimension of folks, all with spare cash who wish to be known as animal people and desire the status species that are the current "hype" of the cocktail circuit. In my time upon the scene I have seen this economy switch from Black Angus to Arabian Horses to Ostriches and to Llamas or other Camelids. The money involved in the various transactions would choke a Brontosaurus and has no relation to the normal animal trading that went on in the regular world of animal husbandry. Veterinarians, in general and to their credit, survived in this litigious world by applying what they knew of animal medicine from vast experience and mostly extensive training. I was no exception...

I grew to appreciate Llamas greatly, though they never touched my love of dogs and horses. As a group they are easily trained due to their ability to understand what their owners wished. That is, if the owners had the intelligence to understand the easily analyzed ingrained feelings of the animals. Mostly the people in the economy I mentioned above did not, though there were a few who showed promise.

The farm where I was on a pine-studded side hill overlooking a very old, small, historically significant New England town. The owners were intelligent Yankees doing a superior job of raising llamas and selling to the aforementioned wealthy group and dealing daily with, as Vets called them, "the funny money bunch". The lady llama stood at ease as I looked at eyes, ears, feet, and legs. I counted nipples and approved of their placement, noted the body conformation looking for significant defects, and I listened to heart and lungs and guts. While the sharp, people-savvy wife commiserated with the gentle beast, the powerful husband, genetically blessed with Yankee capabilities, squeezed the llama against a wood fence as I confirmed her pregnancy by rectal examination. There was a noticeable though unspoken aura of relief as the sale clinching baby was announced and a few thousand of profit assured.

"How about a beer, Doc? It's the days end!", John declared as if the good news were my doing.

"Thanks. As you know I love beer but my day isn't over yet. I sadly replied. "One more stop and then to my cabin."

"Who ya' got stashed there this week?" Nancy, his wise wife, chuckled with an obscene lilt.

"Jes' me and ma dawg."

"Nice," in her eyes a clever glint.

Confident then of real friendship, I left to see the horse over the next ridge.

The sun was low and the shadows long as I topped the ridge. Below me lay a gorgeous valley, in evening light, filled with huge oaks and very old sycamores with tops now lighted briefly by the descending sun. Stone walls, a century old, surrounded neatly cared for meadows that held grazing young cattle. Deer filtered in from the wooded borders to feast after winter on new alfalfa and clover plants. The beauty of this planet stops me cold sometimes and I worry about man's on-going separation from it. That separation results in environmental decisions, sometimes drastic in ignorance..

"Clarence came off the last jump on the cross country course about three legged lame today. God I hope he didn't break something. Please, Doc, fix him or I'll surely die," Sam pleaded.

He stood holding the halter of a huge bay Trakhaner stallion sure enough standing on only three legs. In his great brown eye I could see plenty of pain and some struggle to remember me. We had met often enough but his pain and his owner's anxiety had concerned him enough so that he didn't quite have his world in line yet.

Sam was a tanned, blond, wiry homosexual of extraordinary ability in the training and riding of horses. I had long admired him and Clarence as an equestrian team and had defended them often against obtuse remarks about the relationship from horsemen whose minds wallowed in a machismo mist. Sam weighed in at about one hundred fifty pounds and Clarence at thirteen hundred fifty but, as an athletic pair, they were incomparable. Sam was close to tears and Clarence was frightened by this, used to the emotional level at which they always communicated.

I took the lead shank and talked softly to the big animal and, in a few moments, he relaxed and was ready for me to work. Hoping that I would find nothing, I probed and gently twisted each joint from the shoulder down as I held the leg flexed in my hand. Finding no sign of pain, much to my relief, I straddled the fore leg to examine the foot. Most lameness is found in the foot but protocol in finding the trouble is unchanged. I used hoof testers like large calipers, to put specific pressure on small areas of the hoof over certain anatomical parts. About half way round the inside wall, Clarence removed his foot by standing rapidly on his hind legs and causing my testers to fly against the barn wall. He then looked down at me, somewhat apologetic, but held up a shaking front foot as his anxious eyes showed primitive fire.

"I guess we found the trouble, Sam! He has twisted his shoe and levered one of the nails into the sensitive part of the foot. I couldn't be happier. We'll have him better in two days."

Sam broke into tears and hugged the huge neck. The great horse's head came down as if to calm his partner and they stood for a moment, greatly relieved at the news.

"I will have to block the nerves to the foot in order to pull the shoe but that's no problem, Sam. Clarence is easy to work with and you have helped me before. Let's go," I barked.

Sam snapped to with that mild order and a short time later we had blocked the foot, cut the nails, and pulled the shoe. All the while a placid Clarence munched timothy hay and acted as if it never happened. Sam hugged him again and I shook his hand quickly, afraid he might hug me. This great horseman whispered a tearful thanks and did manage to squeeze my shoulder. No problem!

The nail hole was gently infused with antibiotic gel and I gave Clarence a dinosaur-dose of penicillin in his humungous pectoral muscles. His tetanus vaccines were up to date so I then cleaned up, packed up, and noticed as I waved to Sam that the car clock said six-forty-five. Two oak ridges later I drove through massive white pines, crossed a wooden bridge over a small stream, and came to my cabin on the river-bank amidst quiet, dark green hemlocks. I turned off the car and let my head fall back. There was slow wind movement of the graceful conifer boughs, sounds of geese high in the sky, and a peaceful murmuring of the river around the boulders. I was grateful to be able to see the richness of my fulfilled life and somewhat driven to talk it over with someone aware and strong. People who show strength to give confidence and focus to others do undergo invasive waves of serious loneliness at times. It was shower time for sure!

After a welcome hot shower I returned three calls I got from answering service. All were convinced that Saturday afternoon would be convenient for all. I poured a Scotch that I get to once a week and sat on a bench by the river to wait for the brown haired girl---now, after ten years, more woman in my mind. All the calls, none urgent, were put off to Sunday. A space in time now that was my own! How rare--How wondrous! At that time in my life, solitude was my greatest companion. I did note, however, I was listening for a car and my dog seemed to be also!

The lady arrived a half hour later. She cooked the vegetables and I did the steak over a wood fire. Conversation was unhurried and her ideas, though not always in agreement with mine, had an aura of wisdom and experience. The talk was mostly mine and she listened expertly and commented without hesitance. Neither moved to do the dishes, I noticed, but we loved and slept with serenity and, with morning, my world seemed to have tipped ever so slightly on its axis. ************

CHAPTER TWELVE: Sunday Again

Since childhood, sleep for me never lasts much beyond first light. This has been of value through school, training, medical practice, war, and a lifetime of enjoying fishing and the world at dawn. It's a pleasant biological rhythm and the lady who held me in her embrace had the same pace and I silently thanked my ongoing luck.

"I really should care for my horses and get teenagers in gear," she said quietly, "and I don't care for coffee."

She was dressed and gone rapidly but I had no feeling of being cut short - only one of admiration that she knew her own strong mind and my conviction of her honest love for me. Perhaps that vague new tangent from which I saw the world was permanent and I was pleased to regain familiar solitude.

On Sunday the usual routine was to schedule nothing but to arrange to see any case that experience taught me should be seen either at the farm or the clinic. Usually there was one to be seen and then I would line up whatever else happened based on the time of the most critical case. The routine was good for my clients but had not been really good for family relations. Now in my solitary life it was fine.

The answering service had given me five calls to return and one person I was to see at the clinic at one PM. I had also had arranged to castrate a two year old colt at eleven AM because the owner had time from work then to give me a hand. My social life during these times was hard to separate from my work, as I was always available except, of course, from Tuesday night to Wednesday night. It was then eight AM so I picked up my flyrod and headed down stream.

For a few years I had had an ongoing contest with a brown trout in a back eddy below two boulders only a tad downstream. In about six tries I had hooked him three times and netted him twice. The previous year he was 14 inches and I was anxious to see how he had grown. His good fortune was that I didn't relish the flesh of browns but rainbows and brookies had to be cautious!

I waded in well above the rocks and slowly worked the fly, a large hare's-ear, in the run above the pool, all the time watching it for signs of a feeding fish. My eyes took in cowslips and trout-lilies, my nose the odor of fresh earth and wild azalea while my skin was treated to a warm rising sun and a gently touching breeze. My peripheral vision caught a flash of dull white far down in the deep end of the pool and I let the fly go down with the current only the leader's-length below the boulders to where the fish fed. I stopped the line and as the nymph lifted, it was smashed by my fish and the reel sang as he tore downstream well hooked. The fish fought well but was no match for my three ounces of graphite rod and, of course, my well-honed and treacherous skill (also known as luck). He was a superior trout of fifteen inches and I hope is still in that pool. The day was already triumphant, so I quit and returned to the cabin for a forever evil and consistently welcome coffee and cinnamon bun.

My route to see the colt took me through the center of two villages where the main activity was families going to old white steepled churches. Older people like myself and younger couples with primly groomed children. I saw few younger couples alone, but this scene I looked forward to seeing for I believed in the strength of this Christian world and never spoke against it. I assumed that there truly once was a man named Jesus and he said all the right things. After all, I reasoned, to the gentler and wiser people who could only look forward to savagery, rape, and death hung up on sticks his words were welcome and really caught on. My early life in the Pacific had removed from my mind any hope of his Father, or any one, ever being in control of things, especially someone having all encompassing love. I never speak against the belief, however, as I have seen the good it does when the chips are truly down. I admire the raiments of the church, the bible stories and especially the power of its music sung by strongly believing voices. In temples and cathedrals and gothic churches, I feel as if I were a traitor in their midst, though confident and happy!

*****

"This colt likes to play, Doc. I don't know how you will ever get close to his vein."

This was advice from Bill, the fireball colt's owner and one of the best horsemen I've known. I paid attention and suggested,

"Let's turn him out in the paddock to work off some steam while I get ready."

He concurred and the young animal ran, kicked, leaped, and snorted, all for my benefit as I readied the instruments and scrubbing pail.

"That's all 'cause you're here ya know," Bill said. "I'll never catch the bugger."

"I know," I said thankful of his horse sense," but he's so curious about me he'll come right up and I'll pick him up."

Fortunately it worked and the youngster followed, especially when I walked away from him. With only brief anxiety I soon was able to administer the proper series of drugs and, as he lay on the soft spring earth, I was able to excise his testicles.

Bill and I waited for the colt to awake and he said, "I'm sure glad that's over," as he sighed in relief.

We stood and discussed the confined lonely life an uncut stallion must lead. His libido is such that, in most cases, he must be ridden and kept alone. In a stall he often develops bad habits and a severe frustrated personality. No one ever has time to give him the amount of physical use his power demands.

The dazed animal was soon up and around with no knowledge or memory of what had occurred, and I headed for the clinic.

I had a welcome quiet hour at the clinic answering correspondence and then answered the door for an older lady who brought in her older, ailing, and blind terrier for euthanasia. The lady was shaken and teary but bravely resolute as he went quietly to sleep forever. He had been a gentle and empathetic friend for fourteen years and I advised and she agreed to replace him with a puppy to worry about and to wet the rug. She smiled briefly, touched the little dog's body, and rapidly left.

I cannot catalog the hundreds of differing emotions these times of pet loss produce, but I suspect it was the most important service I ever performed in forty years of practice. Properly done, more important, even, for the humans than for the animals.

Mr. Beel called with two announcements, the first one being that there had been an icy episode of human shunning in his office. His secretary, with competence, had opened his mail and left on his desk, for all to see, a lab report that said, "ANGEL IS PREGNANT". Until he explained that Angel was his horse, this prominent attorney was a social outcast and left me undone with laughter.

Then Mr. Beel outlined how he and two neighbors, also owning large acreage of the most beautiful land in my "Parish', had arranged that it be forever saved from development. They should know of the joy in my heart that two prominent men were conscious of this planet's beauty and had taken action hoping that more would copy.

During the course of the remainder of the finally quiet afternoon, I spoke by phone with a competent attractive young woman who has grown up in the local area and was an especially able horse woman. She was a graduate of a prominent Veterinary college and had been in another Doctor's horse practice in a neighboring state for two years. We were friends and we discussed what her next move should be. The call ended with her agreement to come and talk about her buying my practice. I realized I was pleased with the prospect.

I left my desk and entered the ward where my many patients were kept and I found that checking them all for full water dishes and clean bedding was a pleasant chore.

I was closing the ward door when the phone jangled again.

"WE WON! WE WON! You're great!" was the message loudly proclaimed by a surprisingly jubilant Elisa at the fairgrounds and it really made my day shine.

I felt warmly fulfilled about the previous week and as I was turning out the lights to leave for my cabin the phone rang once more. It was Antonio.

"Sure glad to catch you on a Sunday, Doc." My top cow is calving and I think you better have a look.

"I'll be there. We'll fix her up," I said.

A brief moment later I was headed down my beloved valley in late afternoon shadow------happily needed and competent to serve. I hoped within a year to be married to that brown-haired lady and retire to endless days of Tuesday night to Wednesday night... ..forever.

THE END